FRIENDS

OF

DOROTHY

FOR SYLVAIN

At the time of publication, all URLs printed in this book were accurate and active.
Charlesbridge, the author, and the illustrator are not responsible for the content or accessibility
of any website.

An Imagine Book
Published by Charlesbridge
9 Galen Street
Watertown, MA 02472
(617) 926-0329
www.imaginebooks.net

Library of Congress Cataloging-in-Publication Data
Names: Uzarowski, Anthony, author. | Mogollo Díez, Alejandro, illustrator.
Title: Friends of Dorothy: a celebration of LGBTQ+ icons / Anthony Uzarowski;
    illustrated by Alejandro Mogollo Díez.
Description: Watertown, MA: Charlesbridge, [2023] | Includes bibliographical
    references. | Summary: "A celebration in words and artwork of entertainers and artists
    who have been an inspiration to the queer community."—Provided by publisher.
Identifiers: LCCN 2022025393 (print) | LCCN 2022025394 (ebook)
    | ISBN 9781623543518 (hardcover) | ISBN 9781632892454 (ebook)
Subjects: LCSH: Sexual minorities—Biography. | Celebrities—Biography. | Gays and
    the performing arts.
Classification: LCC HQ75.2 .U93 2023 (print) | LCC HQ75.2 (ebook)
    | DDC 306.76/0922 [B]—dc23/eng/20220912
LC record available at https://lccn.loc.gov/2022025393
LC ebook record available at https://lccn.loc.gov/2022025394

Display type set in Bely Display by Roxane Gataud and
    Trend Sans One by Latinotype
Text type set in StoneSans by Sumner Stone
Printed by 1010 Printing International Limited in Huizhou, Guangdong, China
Production supervision by Jennifer Most Delaney
Design by Nicole Turner

Printed in China
(hc) 10 9 8 7 6 5 4 3 2 1

FRIENDS OF DOROTHY

A CELEBRATION OF LGBTQ+ ICONS

ANTHONY UZAROWSKI

WITH ARTWORK BY
ALEJANDRO MOGOLLO DÍEZ

imagine!

THE ICONS

INTRODUCTION

From classic silver screen goddesses like Judy Garland, Marilyn Monroe, and Marlene Dietrich; through grand divas like Cher, Barbra Streisand, and Liza Minnelli; to modern-day songstresses such as Lady Gaga and Lana Del Rey, the LGBTQ+ community has always had a unique set of iconic patrons. What makes a gay icon? A blend of strength and vulnerability; being at odds with social conventions; and presenting a charismatic, bold, and flamboyant style of performance. All these elements and much more.

There is no set sexual orientation or gender identity required to become an icon for the queer community: It's all about attitude. Free, uninhibited expression, an open mind, creativity,

and bravery—these are just some of the features characterizing the most enduring icons.

Many of our icons were themselves queer. Some, like Marsha P. Johnson or Sylvia Rivera, fought for LGBTQ+ rights. Others, like Divine, Sylvester, or RuPaul, shattered social barriers to become important cultural ambassadors of queerness, changing the world in the process.

Growing up in an ultraconservative environment, I had no idea what a gay icon was. I was a scared and confused kid, bullied by my schoolmates and deeply closeted, convinced I was the only one to feel this way. Throughout my childhood, I was drawn to certain actors and musicians but with no idea they held a special place in the hearts of other queer people. I fell in love with Marilyn Monroe when I was five. I loved Madonna and Cher. I watched *Truth or Dare* in secret, witnessing gay lives represented on screen for the first time. Only later did I discover that the people who in many ways saved me through my childhood were all seen as queer icons—which means that they had done it many times over, for other kids just like me.

For decades we had no queers to look up to; mainstream popular culture pretended we didn't exist. But it was those others—people framed as straight but nonetheless struggling to fit in within the straight narrative, or sometimes outright defying it—who were the ones to give us hope and make us feel less alone. This book is meant as a tribute to them but also to us, a community of survivors. I wasn't able to include all of the iconic figures we've grown to love here; by its very nature, this list is incomplete and subjective. There is no exhaustive, definitive list of queer icons. The bottom line is, whoever helped you when you felt like there was no one in the world who loved or understood you, whoever made you feel seen, or gave you hope for a brighter future—whether through a movie performance, a song, a book, or a poem—they are your queer icons. Here's to them.

JUDY GARLAND

Perhaps the first widely recognized queer icon, Judy Garland's own life mirrored the struggles faced by the community that embraced her. Throughout the many ups and downs of her career as a singer and actress, gay fans stood by her, elevating her status to that of a patron saint for an entire generation. Even in death, her link to the community remained eerily tight, with her funeral taking place mere hours before the Stonewall riots erupted. Today, she remains the quintessential pre-Stonewall gay icon—a surrogate mother and a cultural avatar for those without a voice.

It is impossible to talk of Judy Garland without acknowledging her importance as a queer icon. While certainly not the first cultural figure to be idolized by the members of the LGBTQ+ community, she was the first with a widely recognized following among gay men, and therefore her power as a unifying force in a community which had historically been fragmented and consisted of largely isolated individuals cannot be overestimated. During the Second World War, gay men would start referring to each other as "friends of Dorothy," a nod to Garland's character in The Wizard of Oz, which premiered in 1939, a week before Hitler invaded Poland. It didn't matter if they saw the movie or were fans of Judy—she was the glue that held them together during a time when being outed spelled dishonorable discharge from the army without any benefits enjoyed by other vets.

The Wizard of Oz presented queer audiences with an alternative to the usual heteronormative narratives Hollywood served up. Here was a new kind of kinship and family, one made up of unconventional characters, all trying to navigate their way through a hostile world. Garland's rendition of "Over the Rainbow" became an anthem for a whole generation of LGBTQ+ folks who dreamed of a land, and a time, where they could find acceptance. The song has been credited with helping to popularize the rainbow as a symbol for the community—the beginnings of the rainbow flag so widely recognized today.

In the years after the war, Garland's following only strengthened, as she struggled to stay afloat in the world of Hollywood politics, which she found increasingly challenging. She had been born into show business—her parents were traveling vaudevillians, and little Judy would make her stage debut at the tender age of two when she joined her older sisters to sing "Jingle Bells." Her childhood, such as it was, was marked by hardship and constant performing, and by the time she appeared in *The Wizard of Oz* at age seventeen, she was already considered a veteran. Along the way, the shy teenager suffered abuse at the hands of studio bosses and coworkers. She was shamed for her lack of what was considered movie star looks and for her weight. Louis B. Mayer, the head of MGM, called her his "little hunchback." All this took its toll, and the overworked and overstressed Garland struggled with chronic insomnia, which the studio "cured" with the usual remedy of pills, to which she soon became addicted. As her popularity grew, so did her problems. Throughout the 1940s she was one of MGM's top box office stars, appearing in such classics as *Ziegfeld Girl* (1941), *Babes on Broadway* (1941), *Meet Me in St. Louis* (1944), *Till the Clouds Roll By* (1946), and *Easter Parade* (1948), establishing herself as the biggest musical star of the period. But her talent and popularity never seemed to be enough—in a studio that dealt in manufactured glamour and physical perfection, Garland was always seen as second-best. Her low self-esteem suffered further as a result of disastrous personal relationships. Her parents were domineering and often exploitative, and her romantic life was also turbulent. She dreamed of a family but was actively discouraged from marrying and having children, both by her mother and the studio. It wasn't until 1946 that her marriage to the bisexual director Vincente Minnelli produced her first child, the future queer icon Liza Minnelli, who would make her debut opposite her famous mother just three years later, in the musical *In the Good Old Summertime*.

By the 1950s, although not yet thirty years old, Judy Garland was considered played out. MGM dropped her contract and she struggled to find employment. She went to London and decided to try performing live. When she first appeared at the Palladium in April 1951, she could barely fill the theater. But after the first night's show, the word got around town that something truly magical was taking place. It was on the Palladium stage that Judy Garland graduated from movie star to legend. After that shaky first night, she performed two sold-out shows every evening for the next four weeks, and news of her unprecedented comeback reached as far as Hollywood. It was thanks to her success in London that Judy was able to return to the screen triumphantly with *A Star Is Born* (1954). Alongside *The Wizard of Oz*, it was to become her most iconic role. Her performance as the struggling singer Esther Blodgett, who becomes a major star but struggles to cope with her husband's demons and addiction, is today considered not only Garland's strongest, but is often cited among the best screen performances of all time. Although seen as a major comeback, the film failed to resurrect her movie career, especially as she famously lost the Oscar for Best Actress that year to Grace Kelly. To any queer cinephile, this remains one of the biggest travesties in Hollywood history.

And yet to Garland's fans, of which the most devoted fraction were legions of adoring gay men, she was a living legend and symbol of both the injustice they faced at the hand of society and of survival. As she shifted her focus from films to live concerts, her shows became grand events at which members of the queer community could congregate and relatively openly demonstrate their queerness, at a time when such opportunities were extremely rare. Being gay and being a fan of Judy Garland became inexplicably linked, even if such a connection was reductive and often left large portions of the community out. And yet it is important to acknowledge that, while far from universally inclusive, Garland's queer fandom constituted one of the first widely recognized groups of LGBTQ+ individuals.

A decade later, with her professional and personal life in tatters, she called upon London once more. Again there was the Palladium, and again a legendary triumph, this time alongside her daughter Liza, herself on the verge of major stardom. Garland's voice and delivery were still faultless, and the fragility of her tiny frame and the world-weary quality she now possessed only added to the intoxicating effect she had over her audience. It was also in London that she filmed her last movie, ironically titled *I Could Go On Singing* (1963). In reality, she would never sing on screen again. Physically fragile and financially broke, Judy rented a tiny house in a secluded Chelsea mews and attempted to get her life back on track. There would be more performances, most notably at the Talk of the Town nightclub, where she often appeared on stage more than an hour late, drugged up and barely able to sing. It was clear to anyone who saw her at the club that she needed help, and yet her magic still worked, even under the haze of pills and impending doom. As the English newspaper the *Observer* wrote in January 1969: "She doesn't really give a concert—she conducts a séance. She evokes pity and sorrow like no other superstar." Six months later, she was gone. Almost immediately, Judy Garland the Myth was born. The world was in shock, and the following week, on June 27, more than twenty thousand people gathered outside Manhattan's Frank Campbell Funeral Home to pay their respect to one of the world's greatest entertainers. To them, Judy Garland was more than a singer or a movie star; she was an icon, a unique kind of pop culture martyr. She suffered, she got knocked down, time and time again, and yet she somehow always rose from the ashes of her own misfortune.

Among the vast crowds outside Campbell's, Judy's loyal queer fans stood out. On the day of her funeral, they came in their hundreds to show their love for the woman whose struggles seemed to mirror their own. For some, who never got a chance to see her perform, it was the first time coming together as a community in such a conspicuous manner, in broad daylight, for the world to see.

Later that night, following Garland's memorial, a handful of mourners found themselves at a little gay bar in Greenwich Village. Among them was Sylvia Rivera, a transgender activist, who years later recalled: "I was completely hysterical. The greatest singer, the greatest actress of my childhood is no more. There was no one left to look up to." The bar just happened to be the Stonewall Inn, and this night the place was raided by police, just as it had been countless times before. But unlike all the other nights, this time the queer folk fought back. Although many experts today are skeptical about linking the timing of Garland's funeral with the Stonewall riots, we can never really measure how much influence, if any, the community's grief over the death of their beloved icon had on that night's uprising. In a way, it doesn't really matter. The conjuncture of timing will always remain symbolic: Judy Garland is the quintessential pre-Stonewall icon, and her death signaled the end of an era.

"Wouldn't it be wonderful if we could all be a little more gentle with each other, and a little more loving, have a little more empathy, and maybe we'd like each other a bit more."

JOAN CRAWFORD

Few stars can claim the title "survivor" more deservedly than Joan Crawford. Rising above a childhood of poverty and abuse, she went on to become one of the most successful actors of Hollywood's Golden Age, at once exuding glamour and down-to-earth relatability. Her iron will and ambition led to a decades-long career, making her one of the most enduring of icons. Whether a quintessential 1920s flapper or a fabulously over-the-top 1960s horror queen, Joan Crawford was never anything less than a star.

Along with Bette Davis and Judy Garland, Joan Crawford is one of the original queer icons. As early as the 1940s, long before the gay liberation movement, queer audiences revered Joan Crawford: a star who had overcome her abusive childhood, poverty, the misogyny and sexism of Hollywood, and who constantly reinvented herself in order to thrive as her best self. She was the ultimate survivor.

She started as a dancer and was famously spotted by an MGM scout in the second line of the chorus. Signed to a contract in 1925, her rise to stardom was slow—having neither pedigree nor connections, she relied on her own talent and her ability to capture attention, to stand out from the other hopefuls who descended upon the movie capital during the roaring twenties. She quickly became known as the queen of the Charleston, even catching the eye of F. Scott Fitzgerald, who thought her to be "the best example of the flapper."

Studio bosses also took notice, and Crawford's star was soon on the rise. During the Great Depression Joan's popularity soared, and she began amassing a gay following. She specialized in playing women from the wrong side of the tracks who had to fight their way through the unfair obstacles placed on their path by society, who were wronged by men but who usually came out on top. Her screen roles resonated with the public not only because they reflected universal struggles but because they were deeply rooted in Joan's own story.

She came from nothing, and as one of her biographers put it, her childhood made Marilyn Monroe's humble beginnings seem like a fairy tale. Abandoned by her father as an infant, she was forced to earn her keep from an early age, and she never managed to get past fifth grade. What she lacked in education, she made up in moxie. It was perhaps that quality of resilience and a refusal to be discounted that so endeared her to gay audiences. She was able to take whatever rotten hand life had dealt her and—more than rise above it—was able to triumph. In her early films she used her beauty and sex appeal to navigate the male-dominated world and survive. In *Rain* (1932), she played a prostitute fighting for her dignity and exposing religious hypocrisy, and she was a deliciously bitchy social climber in *The Women* (1939). Who could forget the classic zinger: "There's a name for you ladies, but it isn't used in high society, outside of a kennel."

When MGM released her from her contract after almost two decades, many thought it signaled the end of Crawford's career. She was by now in her forties, way past Hollywood's expiry date for leading ladies, and as if that wasn't enough, she had also been labeled "box office poison" by the Independent Theatre Owners of America. But she came back bigger and better than ever, winning an Oscar for *Mildred Pierce* in 1946, followed by two more nominations, for *Possessed* in 1948 and *Sudden Fear* in 1952. By then, she had acquired the iconic look we still associate with Crawford today: broad shoulders; prominent eyebrows framing large, expressive eyes; and a strong, steely quality, offset by a note of tender vulnerability.

Throughout the 1950s, while most of her contemporaries either struggled to stay afloat or had abandoned the business altogether, Crawford continued to be a major star. Her movies were at the time mostly seen as "women's pictures," and although considered beautiful, she was never quite a sex symbol. She was too threatening, too independent, too reluctant to stroke the male ego. Yet besides her devoted female audience, it was the silent but sizable queer following that helped Crawford stay popular throughout the years.

In 1962 she entered yet another renaissance, appearing for the first time opposite another Golden Age icon, Bette Davis, in the camp horror extravaganza *Whatever Happened to Baby Jane?* The film's success was due in part to the real-life feud between the two stars, which, for the purpose of publicity, was exaggerated out of all proportion. With the film's release, a brand-new genre was born, later branded "grand dame guignol," or "hag horror." Crawford took advantage of the newfound popularity by appearing in a string of other deliciously camp titles, including *Strait-Jacket* (1964) and *Trog* (1970), which would prove to be her last big-screen appearance.

Following her death in 1977, Crawford's reputation suffered greatly. In 1978, Joan's eldest adopted daughter published a shocking memoir, painting her famous mother as an abusive narcissist. The popular perception of Crawford as a grotesque monster was further enhanced by the 1981 film adaptation of *Mommie Dearest*,

"I never go outside unless I look like Joan Crawford, the movie star. If you want to see the girl next door, go next door."

in which Faye Dunaway delivered an infamously camp, over-the-top performance. For years it seemed to be the only way the public was willing to view the iconic star—with one notable exception: the gay community. In this space, Crawford, alongside her archrival Bette Davis, was an untouchable goddess. Her loyal fan base in the queer community remained steadfast even after *Mommie Dearest*—in fact, the film's camp aesthetic only reinforced Crawford's iconic status. Her image has been embraced by drag artists the world over, and for decades she was inarguably one of the most imitated icons—you need look no further than *RuPaul's Drag Race* for numerous references to her.

New generations of film lovers, queer and straight alike, are discovering Joan Crawford anew, free from preconceptions.

While Crawford might no longer be the major gay icon she was thirty years ago, she isn't *Mommie Dearest* anymore either. The new generation of queer film lovers is busy rediscovering her, giving her the appreciation she has been due for decades. Crawford has emerged as a trailblazer: a strong, independent woman and a dedicated professional.

With her personal reputation largely rehabilitated, it's time to go back to what matters most: Joan Crawford was, above all, one hell of an actress. In the majority of her ninety-plus films, she is a force that blazes across the screen like a flash of lightning. To watch a Joan Crawford movie is still an Event with a capital E, a heart-stopping experience, despite more than half a century having passed since her best films were made.

BETTE

DAVIS

"She did it the hard way" reads her tombstone, and boy, did she ever. For half a century she blazed as one of the brightest and toughest stars in Hollywood, inspiring awe in cinemagoers and fear in big studio bosses, creating some of the most charismatic screen performances of all time in the process. For generations of queer audiences, Bette Davis symbolized strength, which came not from her tiny frame but seemingly endless reserves of inner fortitude. With her iconic eyes, unmistakable voice, and cigarette in hand, she continues to serve as one of the most enduring inspirations in the pantheon of queer icons.

What made Bette Davis stand out from other movie stars of her generation was that nothing about her outer appearance suggested a screen goddess. When she first arrived in Hollywood, she was upset to find there was no one at the train station to greet her. In fact, a man was sent by Universal Studios, but after scanning the disembarking passengers, he left empty-handed, later explaining that he saw nobody who looked like an actress. From the beginning, it was to be a fierce battle, and Davis was willing to fight. She resisted typecasting and didn't believe that it was her job to be liked. She saw herself as a storyteller, willing to morph into any character a story demanded: a ruthless bitch, a plain spinster, a cockney gold digger, a willful Southern belle. No role was too big a stretch for her.

Queer audiences adored Davis. Her unique blend of audacity and witty intelligence flew in the face of authority and made her appear ultramodern. She was an outsider and a trailblazer, both on-screen and off. When Warner Bros. failed to deliver scripts she deemed worthy of her talent, she took them to court—a move so courageous at the time that it is today seen as the first significant crack in the previously indestructible structure of the studio system. Although she lost the court battle, she won the war of respect and reputation. Throughout the second half of the 1930s and much of the 1940s no other actor, male or female, could quite match Davis's success. During this time she won two Academy Awards and many more Oscar nominations.

But as the Second World War ended, Bette suddenly found herself on the margins of Hollywood. With the rise of sultry femme fatales like Ava Gardner, Rita Hayworth, and Lauren Bacall, Davis started to fall out of favor with audiences, and for the first time since becoming a star her movies flopped at the box office. Yet just when it seemed that her career was over for good, she staged one of the greatest comebacks in movie history, starring as the larger-than-life theater diva Margo Channing in *All About Eve* (1950). Margo's iconic line "Fasten your seatbelts, it's going to be a bumpy night" entered the queer zeitgeist, and Davis became indistinguishable from her character. *All About Eve* would serve as inspiration for generations of drag artists, who'd employ the movie's savagely quotable one-liners and Margo's instantly recognizable look.

"What's more boring than a queen doing a Judy Garland impression? A queen doing a Bette Davis impression." This quote from the groundbreaking 1970 film *Boys in the Band*, perhaps the first mainstream movie openly celebrating gay men and their lifestyle, clearly showcases just how deeply rooted in gay culture the cult of Bette Davis was. The phenomenon can be traced to as early as the 1930s, but as decades rolled on, rather than diminishing, Davis's status only grew in strength. While the mainstream was reluctant to accept female movie stars past a certain age, queer audiences celebrated the campness of the wave of later-stage movies of their already established icons. Of these, Bette Davis was leading the way. Starting

with the 1962 grand dame guignol classic *Whatever Happened to Baby Jane?*, in which Bette came face to face with her longtime rival and fellow gay icon pioneer, Joan Crawford, Davis's signature scenery-chewing muscles were flexed as never before. Here was a world populated by haunting memories and bitter disappointments, and the characters, rejected by society, had little to fall back on besides their grotesque theatrics and venomous back-and-forths. As the queer community geared up toward more structured rebellion, there was something in the defiance of Davis that, once again, struck a chord with the disenfranchised.

Baby Jane would bring Bette Davis her tenth and final Oscar nomination, and in the years that followed, like her archnemesis Joan Crawford, she continued to star in camp extravaganzas. While none of these matched the success of her previous movies, it didn't matter—Bette Davis was by this point well established as a living legend and a survivor, and her reputation as a queer icon only grew through the years of the gay liberation movement. She was one of the first actresses to be widely parodied and imitated by drag artists, and she was one of the first to see it as a compliment and confirmation of the enormous mark she had made on popular culture.

In later years she suffered from ill health, partly because of her lifelong devotion to cigarettes, which, in true Bette Davis

"It's better to be hated for who you are than to be loved for someone you're not. It's a sign of your worth sometimes, if you are hated by the right people."

fashion, she refused to give up even after suffering a stroke. Like Joan Crawford, she was the subject of a tell-all book penned by her daughter; but unlike Crawford, she lived long enough to suffer the heartbreak that came as a result. As the 1980s rolled in, Davis, though frail, continued to be a regular fixture on late-night talk shows, and she traveled the world, collecting lifetime achievement awards and gladly recounting her legendary life and career. Thanks to Kim Carnes's hit song, "Bette Davis Eyes," she also became an icon for the MTV generation, which delighted her.

When she died in 1989, tributes from all over the globe celebrated her as one of the century's greatest actresses and classic Hollywood's definitive stars. To the queer community, Davis's legacy remains considerable. At a time when gay audiences struggled to find any kind of relatable representation in popular culture, Bette Davis offered the sort of strength and defiance of the patriarchal status quo that made each queer audience member feel just that much more significant. Her films were once viewed by solitary, closeted queers, who'd memorize her iconic lines and mannerisms to use as armor in the hostile world. Today she is celebrated collectively, as new generations of LGBTQ cinephiles discover her vast body of work anew. We are able to see her movies together and view them, and Davis herself, as important artifacts of our cultural story.

MARLENE
DIETRICH

With her first appearance as Lola in *The Blue Angel* in 1930, Marlene Dietrich burst on the scene and became an overnight sensation on both sides of the Atlantic. From the beginning, she challenged society's conventions, bringing the liberated, gender-bending sexuality of prewar Berlin to mainstream consciousness, quickly gaining iconic status among the LGBTQ+ community. Already a legend in her own lifetime, Dietrich was a woman ahead of her time, and she continues to inspire new generations of queer fans with her charisma, witty intelligence, and unparalleled fabulousness.

Marlene Dietrich was synonymous with decadence, and in an extraordinary career that spanned six decades, she set her own standards, disregarding preexisting conventions. Nothing had prepared American audiences of the 1930s for the sexually liberated, brazen German beauty who arrived on their screens. With her very first Hollywood movie, *Morocco* (1930), directed by her mentor, Josef von Sternberg, Dietrich set a clear course that she would follow for the rest of her showbiz reign. In the film's most iconic scene, she appears dressed in a tuxedo, crooning seductively to a room full of spectators, before choosing to plant a lingering kiss on the lips of a female audience member. Dietrich is more than playful in the scene; she asserts her dominance, assuming a role traditionally reserved for men. Her body language is confident, her manner unapologetically flirtatious. Throughout the movie, her persona fluidly moves between femininity and masculinity, never settling for just one or the other, all the while maintaining control.

Although the narrative of *Morocco* is conventional, Marlene's androgynous persona was at the time revolutionary and made her a star, as well as an instant icon for queer audiences. What made her unique was that her off-screen persona was even more outrageous than her movie roles. In an era of manufactured glamour, Dietrich was the real deal. Like fellow celluloid icons Katharine Hepburn and Bette Davis, Dietrich had the personality—and the courage—to outlast the artificiality of Hollywood's studio system and transcend the times she lived in. While she continued to make successful films throughout the 1930s, including such classics as *Shanghai*

Express (1932), *Blonde Venus* (1932), *The Devil Is a Woman* (1935), and *Destry Rides Again* (1939), her personal popularity always transcended her movie fame.

With the rise of Hitler in her native Germany, she was constantly being lured to return home and make movies that would glorify the Nazi regime. Dietrich refused, and in 1939 she renounced her German citizenship and became a naturalized American. Her heroic activities during the Second World War are well documented though perhaps underplayed. More than just speaking out against Hitler, she traveled throughout Europe and North Africa entertaining Allied troops, risking her life on par with the soldiers themselves. She loved servicemen, and she thought of herself as one of them. On the battlegrounds of Europe, Dietrich's legend was solidified: she was equally comfortable wearing a uniform or an ultraglamorous gown as she sang or played the musical saw (the latter a huge hit with the troops).

Following the war, she was decorated for her bravery, both in the United States and in France, which in time she would make her home. While she still made movies, giving acclaimed performances in *Foreign Affair* (1948), *Stage Fright* (1950), *Witness for the Prosecution* (1957), *Touch of Evil* (1958), and *Judgment at Nuremberg* (1961), starting in the 1950s she dedicated herself to a career as a cabaret artiste. For the next two decades, she traveled the world with her act, causing a sensation wherever she appeared, drawing crowds to her concerts. Many of her fans were queer. Some had loved her since *Blue Angel*; like them, she was a fearless survivor. Others represented a new generation of LGBTQ fandom. Despite being a star of the golden age of Hollywood, Marlene's progressive approach to sex and life in general meant that she never appeared as a relic of the past, but rather as a trailblazer for a more liberated future.

She also refused to conform in her personal life. At a time when any hint of a scandal had the potential to ruin a career, Dietrich was defiantly unconventional. Although she remained married to Rudolf Sieber, whom she had wed in 1923, the two led largely separate lives, and throughout hers, Marlene was famous for her numerous love affairs with both men and women. What's more, she refused to make a big deal of her bisexuality, never denying it. She once told a journalist, "In Europe, it doesn't matter if you're a man or a woman—we make love to anyone we find attractive."

As Dietrich's legend grew, fed by the now-iconic look she had employed for her live performances, she became a favorite inspiration for drag artists the world over. But her standing with the queer community

"I am, at heart, a gentleman."

went much further back. As an aspiring cabaret act in 1920s Berlin, she was already a favorite of nonconformists. She attended drag balls, dressed up in men's clothes, and openly paraded around the city's many gay-friendly venues in the company of her woman lovers.

Even into her seventies, she maintained a highly glamorous and sexual persona, shattering yet another stereotype and proving that a woman's allure does not carry an expiration date. In her last years, she withdrew from public life and retired to her apartment in Paris, from which she kept up her many friendships and a busy social life mainly via telephone. In death,

she was finally brought home to her beloved Berlin, a place where, in the years following her war activities, she remained a polarizing figure.

Marlene Dietrich remains a relevant icon for queers, representing strength and a disregard for small-minded conventionality. Her contribution to the arts, both through her movie performances and stage legacy, is impossible to overlook. Her presence is still felt in popular culture, where she serves as inspiration for artists ranging from Madonna to Lady Gaga, and her timeless persona is still very much alive within the LGBTQ+ community.

KATHARINE
HEPBURN

Independent, forward-thinking, and unconventional, Katharine Hepburn was a true original, and she remains the reigning queen of the screen two decades after her death. Throughout her long career, she maintained a persona that represented the modern woman, unafraid to challenge traditional notions of femininity and always projecting her bold, unapologetic individuality. An outspoken supporter of liberal causes, Hepburn often risked making enemies in the ultraconservative America of the period. Yet she never wavered. With her androgynous look, strong on-screen image, and unorthodox personal life, Katharine Hepburn remains one of the original LGBTQ+ icons.

Katharine Hepburn was full of contradictions. Although undoubtedly one of the most widely known personalities of the twentieth century, with volumes written about her life and work, she remains somehow elusive. From the early days of her screen career, she escaped categorization, never fitting into any of the molds Hollywood had in place. Undeniably beautiful, she was never considered a bombshell. She was athletic, angular, and in her early films often masculine—highlighting her androgynous features—which no doubt accounted for the fact that she was one of the earliest icons for both gay and lesbian audiences. And yet she could also appear more conventionally feminine, as she did in many of her movies of the 1940s. She challenged the notions of traditional gender roles and the institution of marriage, and yet she constituted one half of the most celebrated cinematic couple of the classical period. She became a feminist icon while refusing to identify as a feminist. This enigmatic, hard-to-pin-down quality is perhaps the very reason Hepburn's appeal has endured for so long.

Born to a progressive, well-to-do family, Hepburn was encouraged to form her own independent opinions from an early age. She attended college, earning a degree from Bryn Mawr, and yet the only future she envisaged for herself was that of an actress. After a few years of struggling on Broadway, she found her true calling when she was discovered by a Hollywood talent scout and put in front of a movie camera. From her very first movie, *A Bill of Divorcement* (1932), it was clear that she possessed the unique quality of a star— and she immediately became one. But her early film career was anything but smooth.

She was naturally drawn to projects that highlighted her tomboyish qualities, and her appearances in movies such as *Christopher Strong* (1933)—directed by the legendary lesbian director Dorothy Arzner, in which she played a female aviator—or the gender-bending *Sylvia Scarlett* (1935), in which she played a young woman in drag, made her immensely popular with the largely closeted queer population. Mainstream audiences and critics disliked this unsettlingly nonbinary Hepburn.

But even in her more conventional incarnations of the period, Hepburn managed to manifest a kind of ambiguous sexuality and confidence that distinguished her from other female stars of the era, particularly from fellow American leading ladies. While European exports like Dietrich and Garbo were allowed to be more daring in their on-screen projection of nonconformist sexuality, the public was far less forgiving of the homegrown talent. But Hepburn never asked for forgiveness; she simply existed, and while in private she often longed for more wide-ranging popularity and acceptance, to her public it seemed that she couldn't care less about what anyone thought of her. She nonetheless achieved mainstream success with early films like *Morning Glory* (1933), for which she won her first Academy Award; *Little Women* (1933); and *Alice Adams* (1935),

but by the end of the decade she was labeled box office poison and had to fight her way back to the top. In the 1940s she found renewed popularity, reinventing herself as a more sophisticated, modern woman. She was unforgettable as Tracy Lord in *The Philadelphia Story* (1940), which allowed her unique qualities to shine for the first time. This newly established image was perfectly utilized and further enhanced by the romantic comedy *Woman of the Year* (1942), which paired her with Spencer Tracy for the first time. The coupling turned out to be a magical combination, and the two would begin an off-screen partnership, which lasted until Tracy's death in 1967. Despite their widely publicized love affair, Tracy remained married to his wife, and he and Hepburn would never live together. In recent years, some have questioned the exact nature of their relationship, suggesting that they were both in fact gay, and that their bond was based on close friendship rather than romantic love.

Throughout her life, Hepburn was rumored to have been bisexual, and over the years she was linked to many different women with whom she supposedly had relationships of varying lengths. Hepburn herself never confirmed this, and her public persona and cinematic image were enough to solidify her status as a nonconforming queer icon, regardless of the exact details of her personal life.

"I have not lived as a woman. I have lived as a man. I've just done what I damn well wanted."

In the 1950s and '60s, at an age when most stars begin to fade, Hepburn reached new heights in her acting career, appearing in such beloved classics as *The African Queen* (1951), *Pat and Mike* (1952), *Guess Who's Coming to Dinner* (1967), and *The Lion in Winter* (1968), the last two both winning her Best Actress Oscars. She also starred in the controversial 1959 adaptation of Tennessee Williams's *Suddenly, Last Summer*, in which she brilliantly portrayed the ultimate domineering mother of a gay poet. The horrific tale, which also featured Elizabeth Taylor and Montgomery Clift, reflected the era's negative attitudes toward homosexuality, but it also signified the first time a complex queer narrative was featured in a mainstream Hollywood movie.

Throughout the later years of her career, Hepburn continued to strengthen her queer following through powerful portrayals of eccentric characters who often struggled to adjust to the heteronormative model of life, particularly where romantic relationships were concerned. She continued to work successfully into old age in film, theater, and television. In 1982, at the age of seventy-five, she won her fourth Oscar for her performance in *On Golden Pond*, setting a still-unbroken record for the most awarded actor in the academy's history.

When Katharine Hepburn died in 2003, she was already regarded as a national treasure and a cultural icon. She remains the ultimate symbol of independence, an emancipated woman who challenged gender stereotypes and lived life exactly the way she wanted.

TALLULAH
BANKHEAD

Tallulah Bankhead might have never enjoyed the same level of screen success as the celluloid goddesses gracing the previous pages, but that didn't stop her from securing a truly iconic status among an entire generation of queer followers—and with her outrageous antics and over-the-top, campy persona, she remains a legend of notoriety. Blessed with both talent and beauty and born into privilege, it was almost inevitable that she should become a star. But from the beginning, Tallulah was more interested in enjoying life and all it had to offer rather than building a successful career. At a time when Hollywood movies were stifled by the prudish rules imposed by the Production Code, Tallulah Bankhead followed her own set of rules, chief of which was to pay no mind to what anyone might say or think of her.

Tallulah Bankhead was one of the most successful stage actors of her generation, and yet it was her personality and outrageous reputation that made her famous and still assures her iconic status. She was outspoken about matters of sex and . . . well, just about everything else. At a time when popular culture was shaped by taboo, she adhered to none. While such gutsiness made it difficult for her to find success in the mainstream, particularly in Hollywood, it was precisely her defiance of society's norms that prompted the queer community to embrace the cult of Tallulah from the earliest days of her career.

Born into one of the most influential political dynasties of the South, throughout her life she faced the disapproval of her conservative family as well as that of the general public. But even in childhood,

Tallulah showed no will to conform. The loss of her mother just days after her birth left a painful void that haunted her for the rest of her life but also shaped her strong character and independence. Determined to escape the constraining environment of the South, she entered a magazine contest which, based solely on her photo, she won. That allowed her to move to New York City at the tender age of fifteen. Though she wanted to be an actress, her unabashed personality and sexual adventures rather than her acting talent established her reputation. During those early New York days she discovered her attraction for both sexes and explored everything the buzzing city had to offer.

Her stage career took off in 1922 when she moved to London, where she quickly became the toast of the town. Her wild

BORN: TALLULAH BROCKMAN BANKHEAD, JANUARY 31, 1902, HUNTSVILLE, ALABAMA

DIED: DECEMBER 12, 1968, NEW YORK CITY

parties and bon vivant lifestyle made her a favorite of the British press, but unlike back home, her reputation didn't stand in the way of professional success. After nearly a decade in London, she returned to America and decided to give Hollywood a try. She had all the ingredients for stardom, and the more liberal atmosphere of the precode years suited her persona. But from the start, she seemed ill-equipped to deal with the hurdles of the movie capital. The films she was offered did little to showcase her talent and bombed at the box office. Tallulah was bored with the Hollywood set, and, aside from her legendary parties, about which people dared to talk only in hushed whispers, she considered her time there wasted.

In 1933 she returned to Broadway, where her reputation as a queer icon began to form. She originated the role in *Forsaking All Others*, which later became a film starring Joan Crawford in Bankhead's role, as well as in *Jezebel* and *Dark Victory*, the film versions of which brought much acclaim to Bette Davis. She harbored little resentment toward her Hollywood rivals—by this point, it seems, Bankhead had reconciled herself to the idea that she would never be a major movie star, and in any case she preferred her status as an outrageous celebrity. She would win acclaim for her acting—significantly for her stage performances in *The Little Foxes* (Bette Davis would again be cast in the film version) and *The Skin of Our Teeth*, as well as

in Alfred Hitchcock's 1944 film *Lifeboat*, which remains her best-known movie. But for the rest of her life, it was Tallulah's myth that fascinated the public much more than any one role she played on stage or screen. By 1950 her legend was already well-established enough for her to serve as an inspiration for the larger-than-life character of Margo Channing in *All About Eve*. Of course, it was Bette Davis who famously brought Margo to life, but Bankhead delighted in telling anyone who'd listen that the character had been based on her, and indeed, Davis's appearance in the movie, down to the wardrobe, seems to support this.

The queer community loved Tallulah because her persona flew in the face of the conservative society of the period. She refused to apologize for her lifestyle and her fluid sexuality, never denying reports of her many love affairs with both men and women—in fact, she delighted in fueling the rumors. "My father warned me about men and booze, but he never said anything about women and cocaine," she once quipped. While her liberated attitude probably cost her more than one professional opportunity, she was too much of a free spirit to conform.

Tallulah Bankhead died in December of 1968, just months before the Stonewall riots. A sensual adventuress who forged her own path at a time when few dared to do so, she continues to symbolize defiance.

"My father warned me about men and booze, but he never said anything about women and cocaine."

JOSEPHINE BAKER

Josephine Baker rose above the constraints of Jim Crow America to become one of the most celebrated women of her time. Renowned across the world for her unmistakable look and style of dance, she shattered barriers and established herself as a shining beacon of hope for an entire generation of African Americans. Bisexual and famously liberated, she also carried the torch for the LGBTQ+ community, particularly for Black queers, who often felt even more invisible and suppressed than those in the community who benefited from white privilege. Baker never wavered in her battle for equality, whether dancing the Charleston in her banana skirt or marching for civil rights, and she remains one of the most inspirational icons.

Growing up in St. Louis in the early years of the twentieth century, Josephine Baker witnessed first-hand the racism that permeated the country. Decades later, speaking at the historic March on Washington, she recalled the early, traumatizing events of those formative years filled with hardship. By the time she was twenty, she had already been married and divorced twice. At a time when intense segregation meant that finding steady employment in the entertainment industry verged on impossible, especially for a woman, Josephine was determined to succeed. She traveled to New York City while still in her teens and quickly established a name for herself as a talented dancer, a charismatic personality, and something of a clown. While in later life she would repeatedly maintain that she never found success until after she had left the United States, in truth by 1925 she was enjoying a fairly successful career as a dancer in a variety of New York shows. It was clear, however, that as a woman of color, there was only so far she'd be allowed to progress. When an opportunity presented itself for Baker to travel to Paris, she jumped at the chance, sensing that a whole new world was about to open before her.

In Paris she became an almost instant hit, with her distinctive beauty and provocative dance style perfectly tuned to the mood of the time. With African art highly fashionable, many regarded Josephine Baker as a living embodiment of the Black statues that graced the drawing rooms of the Parisian elite. She performed a notoriously legendary number, wearing little more besides a skirt of bananas, putting herself in control of her racial heritage, her sexuality, and any preconceived notions audiences might have had. She soon added singing to her repertoire, and she thus became one of the most beloved chanteuses of the era. Her recording of "*J'ai Deux Amours*" would remain her signature song for the rest of her career.

With her sensational success in France, Josephine Baker became one of the most recognizable names in the world and the first Black woman to enjoy star status across different cultures and countries. News of her achievements crossed the Atlantic, and her name alone began to symbolize Black pride. For those growing up Black and queer, Baker was perhaps the first icon to carry hope: she was not only successful and glamorous but also unapologetically androgynous in her appearance and sexual in her art, as well as nonconformist in her private life. Rumors of her love affairs with members of both sexes started as early as the 1930s and throughout the years would link her with such legendary names as Frida Kahlo, the French novelist Colette, and the jazz vocalist Ada "Bricktop" Smith.

In 1936 Baker returned to the United States to appear in the legendary Ziegfeld Follies on Broadway, and though she was a world-renowned star, her attempt to bring her act home ended in heartache. She was reminded of why she had chosen to leave a decade earlier and was devastated to discover that the country's racist attitudes had worsened, prompting her to return to France. The following year she renounced her American citizenship and became a French citizen. The French embraced her as a national icon, a status reinforced by Baker's heroic war record. Throughout the Second World War she was active in the French resistance, gathering information and carrying secret messages concealed in her sheet music, and she also toured, entertaining the troops. For her courage she was later named a chevalier of the legion d'honneur, France's top honor.

Following the war years, Baker made a triumphant return to the Parisian stage and subsequently toured the world, greeted everywhere she went as a living legend. Her act became increasingly camp, incorporating elaborate costumes and flamboyant aesthetics. But alongside her career, she never ceased to fight for equality, and although no longer an American citizen, throughout the 1950s and '60s she was one of the most vocal supporters of the civil rights movement. Her activism culminated in her appearance alongside Martin Luther King at the March on Washington in 1963, where she famously declared:

I have walked into the palaces of kings and queens and into the houses of presidents. And much more. But I could not walk into a hotel in America and get a cup of coffee, and that made me mad. And when I get mad, you know that I open my big mouth. And then look out, 'cause when Josephine opens her mouth, they hear it all over the world.

"We must change the system of education and instruction. Unfortunately, history has shown us that brotherhood must be taught when it should be natural."

In addition to her activism, Baker was dedicated to bringing equality and hope to her own home. She adopted twelve children from diverse backgrounds, creating what she called the "Rainbow Tribe." Though the experiment proved to be a huge strain on her finances and on her emotional ability to juggle motherhood with the demands of her stage career, she was proud of her pioneering efforts and continued to believe that her "tribe" was proof of the fact that people of different backgrounds and skin colors can live together in peace and harmony. While famously bisexual and liberal in her own approach to sexuality, Baker was said to have been less tolerant with her own children, reportedly sending one of her sons to live with his adoptive father after discovering that he was gay. This little-known fact leaves something of a blemish on her reputation as a queer icon, although she is by no means the only person with an extensive gay following to have demonstrated homophobic behavior.

Whatever her personal feelings about members of the LGBTQ community—her own community—Baker died enjoying the undisputed status of a beloved icon, cherished by drag artists and queers from different racial and cultural backgrounds, credited for smashing barriers and contributing to the creation of a more equal and more accepting world.

MAE WEST

Mae West single-handedly revolutionized sex and the ways in which it was depicted in American cinema—but more than that, she herself was a revolution. Beginning in vaudeville and then on the New York stage, West established herself as a raunchy, sometimes scandalous performer, unapologetically tackling such taboo topics as homosexuality and premarital sex. By the time she made her Hollywood debut she was nearly forty, but that didn't stop her from quickly becoming one of America's top stars. West was an original. Often copied but never to be duplicated, she owned her sexuality and navigated the man-dominated business very much on her own terms. Decades after her death, she remains a favorite among drag artists, thanks to her instantly recognizable style and iconic, innuendo-laden one-liners.

Long before Madonna and Cher, even before Marilyn Monroe, there was Mae West. The original scandal queen, her name was synonymous with sex and the tantalizing promise of the forbidden. If West lacked the beauty of Dietrich or Garbo, she more than made up for it in attitude and wit. Where most of her fellow stars of the period were the creation of visionary directors and big studios, Mae West was the product of her own vision—she created her own plays and scripts and was always fully in control of her image. Her frankness and lighthearted attitude toward sex was a breath of fresh air at a time when censorship was beginning to squeeze real life out of motion pictures. West knew how to trick the censors, and her ability to spike her scripts with double entendres and suggestive phrases became legendary.

Although today mostly remembered as a movie star, Mae West had already enjoyed a highly successful stage career before she made her first picture. Born in Brooklyn, she was determined to make it into showbiz from an early age, and she worked her way up through various vaudeville shows before establishing herself as a racy performer in her own right. She was heavily influenced by drag artists and female impersonators, whose exaggerated looks and risqué humor suited her own image far more than that of typical female acts of the period. She was soon writing her own plays, often under a pseudonym. Encouraged by her success, she injected more spice into each new character. In 1926, Mae wrote a play simply entitled *Sex*. The outraged editors of the New York papers refused to carry ads for the play, which nonetheless became a huge success. The show's popularity soared even further after she was arrested on obscenity charges. She spent eight days in prison, reportedly drinking and dining with the wardens each night and wearing her pure silk underwear the entire time. When she returned to her play, she was a bona fide star.

Her next show would prove even more scandalous. *The Drag* was West's tribute to her many gay friends, and it openly dealt with issues of homosexuality and discrimination. West held auditions for the play at a Greenwich Village gay bar, and most of the actors cast were indeed queer—unheard of at the time. The show, which culminated in a full-on drag ball, proved too controversial for Broadway, and after a few out-of-town performances it was forced to close. The closure did not prevent queer audiences from noticing West, however, and she became one of the earliest allies for a community that otherwise had no public platform of its own.

After the success of her play *Diamond Lil*, Mae was finally persuaded to try her luck in Hollywood. At an age when most actresses considered retirement, she burst onto the screens as an earthy, sexually charged, larger-than-life bombshell in *Night After Night* (1932). Although she only had a supporting role, she managed to con-vince the studio to let her rewrite her dialogue so that it better suited her already established persona. The film proved a great success, and it led to a lucrative contract with Paramount Studios, where for the next six years she made some of the most successful movies of the time. She claimed to have discovered Cary Grant by spotting the handsome young actor through the window of her studio dressing room, and she insisted he be cast opposite her in *She Done Him Wrong* (1933). The film launched Grant's career and firmly established West as America's most notori-ous, and most popular, sex symbol. Based on *Diamond Lil*, the film perfectly showcased the persona she had spent years creating. It also constitutes a lasting testament to her skill as a writer, with the film's most famous line, "Why don't you come up and see me sometime?" entering the lexicon of queer culture.

West continued to blaze through the 1930s with a succession of films, each of which pushed the boundaries of what was acceptable to the very brink. With such classics as *I'm No Angel* (1933), *Belle of the Nineties* (1934), *Klondike Annie* (1936), and *My Little Chickadee* (1940), West assured her place among the most popular movie stars of Hollywood's golden age. She also continued to strengthen her popularity

"It's better to be looked over than overlooked."

among queer audiences, who saw in her the symbol of defiance and disregard for the stifling moral norms of the era. She was also one of the first motion picture stars to acknowledge, and embrace, her queer following. As the popularity of her films began to dwindle, she moved back to the stage, where her shows, which often featured lines of muscle hunks wearing little more than their underwear, drew crowds.

In her later years, West became something of a recluse, spending most of her time in her white and gold apartment in Hollywood, but she still made occasional appearances on the radio, on stage, and on TV. She also returned to the big screen in the 1970s, with roles in *Myra Breckinridge* (1970) and *Sexette* (1978)—both of which became camp classics, despite being unsuccessful at the time. West never stopped being a star, and she never let go of her persona as the larger-than-life, highly sexual, witty dame who commanded any room she entered—and instantly owned any man she came across.

FRIDA
KAHLO

During her lifetime Frida Kahlo struggled to be understood and appreciated, but in the decades following her death, her art and personal style became iconic, making Kahlo one of the most recognizable artists in history. Nonconforming and acutely sensitive to the struggles of others, as well as uniquely tuned to her own inner world, from the beginning Kahlo and her art appealed to the queer community. The visual iconography associated with her life and work continues to evoke all the beauty and torment of a misunderstood artist.

While she was living, Frida Kahlo was rarely seen as much more than an eccentric personality and the wife of the great Mexican artist Diego Rivera. Although she worked steadily throughout her life, creating around two hundred paintings and exhibiting work in the United States and France as well as her native Mexico, it wasn't until the 1970s, long after her death, that Frida's significance as an influential artist and a woman ahead of her time began to be appreciated. It is also around this time that her image started being used by the LGBTQ+ community as a symbol of the defiant outsider and an example of a gender-bending artist whose potential had been suppressed by the power of patriarchy. Her status as a queer icon was also reinforced when the first full-length biographies appeared in the late seventies, suggesting that the troubled painter was most probably bisexual. Since then, she's been linked to many iconic women, including Josephine Baker, fellow painter Georgia O'Keeffe, and Hollywood star Dolores del Rio.

Born in Mexico City, Frida would spend much of her artistic life celebrating her national heritage and culture, incorporating many of its elements into her work. Aside from Mexican folklore, her painting would be heavily infused with Kahlo's personal traumas, most predominantly with her experience of chronic pain. As a young woman, Frida sustained serious injuries in a bus accident, which resulted in a lifetime of physical pain and a multitude of health problems. In her depictions of her own body and the suffering she experienced, she broke new ground in the way female artists were allowed to present their bodies and their stories of what it meant to be a woman. Among her paintings, the numerous self-portraits are most notable and most iconic. While art theorists continue to try to define Frida's work as either surrealist or part of the magical realism movement, the truth is that Frida Kahlo's style is unique, escaping precise classification or definition. "They thought I was surrealist," she wrote. "I wasn't. I never painted dreams. I painted my own reality."

Kahlo's paintings fetch millions at auction houses around the world, but during her own lifetime she struggled to be taken seriously as an artist. That she was female was part of the reason, but also that her style was experimental and emotional— the very qualities that would eventually establish her as one of the most iconic artists of the century. Another obstacle to overcome was the shadow cast by her husband, Diego Rivera, at the time the leading figure in Mexican art. The two first met when Frida was a teenager and Rivera had come to paint a mural at her school. Years later they reconnected at a party thrown by the photographer Tina Modotti. Frida was by then a member of the Communist Party, as was Rivera, and they quickly bonded over mutual love of Mexican art and socialist ideology. Their relationship was tumultuous, filled with infidelity on both parts, and they would divorce and remarry, eventually remaining together until Frida's death.

Although Frida traveled to the United States and later to Europe, where she became the toast of Paris, she always came back to her beloved Mexico.

Wearing a traditional Mexican dress and flowers in her hair, she is today perhaps the best-recognized Mexican, her fame far exceeding that of her husband's. If in life she often had to struggle with the limitations imposed on her by the sexist standards of the time, as well as by her own disability, her posthumous popularity and status as an icon stem from her inner fortitude and refusal to let herself be defeated by adversity. It is also her unique blend of feminine beauty and masculine elements, which she often mixed both in her art and in her personal style and attitude, that has endeared her to the queer community.

But the queerness of Frida's art goes deeper than the androgynous depictions of her self-portraits; the way she was able to translate her own pain and isolation into the language of art remains unique and starkly modern. In her work, Kahlo played with imagery, employing social critique, questioning gender roles and oppressive and exploitative societal structures. Her work remains highly intimate and emotionally charged, transmitting messages of pain and hope in equal measure.

"Feet, what do I need you for if I have wings to fly?"

BILLIE
HOLIDAY

Her life was marred by hardship, addiction, and abuse, but Lady Day managed to rise above it all and establish herself as one of the most celebrated vocalists of all time. With unforgettable songs, such as her groundbreaking recording of "Strange Fruit," Holiday defined Black pride and went on to symbolize both the beauty and the suffering of her people. More than half a century after her death, her music and image continue to inspire, and she is forever an icon of perseverance and the triumph of talent and courage in the face of adversity.

There are few voices as instantly recognizable and as widely loved as that of Billie Holiday. Even for those who aren't connoisseurs of jazz and blues, Holiday's unique, melancholic delivery and heart-wrenching vocal make her recordings irresistibly hypnotic. Her unquestionable talent and the earthy quality of hard-lived experience she brings to every lyric resonate with listeners of all ages, transcending generations and cultures.

Born in Philadelphia, Holiday would spend her troubled childhood in Baltimore, where she was subjected to physical and sexual abuse, child labor, and racial prejudice. She and her mother moved to Harlem in 1929, where she experienced more trauma, including being forced to perform sexual favors in exchange for money to help her mother financially. After being arrested on vagrancy charges at the age of fourteen, Holiday decided that music would be her way out of her bleak reality. By eighteen, she had made her first recording and was on her way to becoming one of the most acclaimed jazz singers of her time. While success came quickly, systemic racism was impossible for Holiday to ignore. Working with Artie Shaw's all-white band, she was often unable to stay in the same hotel or eat in the same restaurant as her bandmates, despite being the star of the show. After being asked to ride in a separate elevator in a New York hotel, Holiday quit the band. Soon after, she recorded what was to become one of her most iconic songs, "Strange Fruit." Written by Abel Meeropol, its lyrics described lynching, and while the song was considered controversial at the time of its release, it became Holiday's first hit, and it went on to be regarded as a monumental event in the history of Black music.

Despite her success and celebrity status, Holiday remained true to her roots. She was known for her salty language and tough, no-nonsense manner, which was tempered by deep sadness and vulnerability. She also refused to conform to social norms of the time, openly living her life as a bisexual woman (another queer icon, Tallulah Bankhead, was among her love interests). But ultimately, it was Holiday's relationships with abusive men that spelled her downfall. She was drawn to violent and abusive characters, and by the 1940s she also became addicted to alcohol and drugs, including heroin. Her personal life became a series of disasters, including several arrests on drug possession charges, and her career suffered.

But the public loved Billie Holiday despite, or perhaps because of, her personal troubles, which she was able to weave into her music quite unlike any other artist. Her iconic recordings include "Lover Man," "That Ole Devil Called Love," and "Don't Explain," the last of which she wrote after catching her husband cheating on her. In 1947, at the peak of her commercial success, Billie was arrested for possession of drugs, and after an infamous trial at which she appeared without legal representation, she was sent to prison, where she stayed until the following year. The incident left her traumatized and didn't prevent her from falling back into addiction. Yet she made a triumphant comeback with her legendary performance at Carnegie Hall in 1948 and continued to record acclaimed albums.

The 1950s brought more personal heartache and professional decline, although Billie was by then considered a legendary performer and one of the most talented jazz singers in the world. In 1956 she published a ghostwritten autobiography entitled *Lady Sings the Blues*, which would later serve as the basis for a biopic starring Diana Ross in an Oscar-nominated performance. While the book is today often seen as a sanitized version of her story, no doubt due to the realities of 1950s America, it is still a unique insight into the life and struggles of Holiday as a Black woman before the peak of the civil rights movement.

To Black queer folk, Billie Holiday embodied their anguish. To the LGBTQ+ community at large, her melancholic songs, in which she often sings of impossible or unrequited love, represented an identifiable voice: someone who understood what it meant to be discarded and invisible. In that sense, she is a unique icon, able to bridge the gap between various factions of the queer community, which was historically often deeply fragmented, especially in the early years of the gay liberation movement. Long before the Black disco queens of the 1970s, she stood as a unifying force, universally loved by all.

"I've been told nobody sings the word 'hunger' like I do. Or the word 'love.'"

She died in 1959 at age forty-four, her body marked by years of hardship and abuse. At the time of her death, she was penniless and once again facing a criminal charge for the possession of drugs. In the decades that followed, her stature as a major cultural icon and a musical genius continued to grow. Today, she is still celebrated as a timeless artist, a unique presence on the musical landscape of the past century, and a fierce representative of both the African American and the queer communities.

MARILYN MONROE

A star, a sex symbol, an actress, an icon—to call Marilyn Monroe any of these alone, or even all at once, seems reductive. She was all that, and much more besides. To people around the globe, she continues to constitute a unique symbol of both beauty and tragedy. A talented performer and a complicated, highly sensitive woman, Marilyn redefined Hollywood stardom, elevating it to new heights of glamour, making herself available to ordinary people and always identifying with her public more than she did with the powers that be. As a woman ahead of her time, often misunderstood and victimized by the system, Marilyn has been an important and much-beloved figure for the LGBTQ+ community from the onset of her career, and she continues to occupy a central spot in the pantheon of queer icons.

Marilyn Monroe's story has been told and retold count-less times, and yet she seems to arouse endless fascination. More than six decades after her death, new gener-ations still find in her a source of inspir-ation. In the 1950s, when she first exploded into public consciousness, members of the queer community were among the first to take Marilyn to their hearts. While from the beginning she symbolized hetero-sexual desire, as the ultimate object of the male gaze, it quickly became apparent that she concealed a far more complex persona than that of just another Holly-wood starlet. Her unwillingness to fit the mold the industry tried so hard to force upon her made her an instant icon for those who themselves struggled to find their place in society. As her fame grew, so did her discontent, as she strived to be taken seriously as an artist and a person.

Marilyn's childhood itself has become the stuff of legend. She grew up lonely, most likely abused, in a series of foster homes and orphanages. At sixteen, she was married off to a neighbor's son, James Daugherty, and although she was emo-tionally unprepared for the role of a wife, it was a preferred alternative to being returned to the orphanage. The marriage didn't last long. When the United States entered World War II, Daugherty enlisted in the navy. While he was overseas, his young wife found work in a plane factory, where, while folding parachutes, the future Marilyn Monroe was discovered by a photographer who had been sent to the factory to take pictures of women partici-pating in the war effort. Young Norma

Jean had a star quality instantly captured by the camera. She projected a kind of inner light that was to become part of her legend.

Over the next few years, she transformed herself from a poor orphan to the most glamorous woman in Hollywood—a status cemented by 1953, after she appeared in three consecutive star-making vehicles: the lavish technicolor thriller *Niagara*, the queer-tinted musical *Gentlemen Prefer Blondes*, and the comedy *How to Marry a Millionaire*, opposite Betty Grable and Lauren Bacall. A year before, she had also caused a scandal when nude photos she had posed for some years earlier were published in a calendar. Rather than destroying her career, as some predicted, the story propelled Marilyn, who refused to deny or be ashamed by it, to superstardom. In 1955 she appeared in *The Seven Year Itch*, which features perhaps the most iconic scene in all of cinematic history: Marilyn, wearing a white dress, standing above a subway vent, which tantalizingly blows her skirt up.

Though her movies proved immensely popular with the public, Marilyn's personal appeal established her as a cultural phenomenon. Beyond beauty and sex appeal, she exuded a unique blend of vulnerability and witty intelligence that allowed her to play with her own image of the slightly ditzy blonde to the full effect. But while she owed her initial success to her various incarnations

of the dumb blonde persona, she soon grew tired of repeatedly playing the same character and set out to prove that she was a serious actress. Abandoning Hollywood and Twentieth Century Fox, as well as her marriage to baseball legend Joe DiMaggio, she moved to New York, where with photographer Milton Greene she established her own production company, and began to study acting with Lee Strasberg. Marilyn's emancipation and a quest for independence and respect further enhanced her iconic status among queer followers. Like many in the LGBTQ+ community, she had to fight her way through patriarchy without the support system of a family, relying solely on her own strength.

Following her move to New York—where aside from acting classes she discovered psychoanalysis, befriended poets and artists, and married Arthur Miller, the country's most renowned dramatist—Marilyn returned to Hollywood to make *Bus Stop* (1956), which proved once and for all that she was a gifted actor. Lee Strasberg confirmed this, once stating that in all his experience of working with actors, he had only twice come across true greatness: with Marlon Brando and Marilyn Monroe. Despite critical success with her work in *Bus Stop*, she was snubbed at the Academy Awards—in fact, she would never earn a single nomination. She was to complete only four more movies:

"We are all born sexual creatures, thank God. It's a pity so many people despise and crush this natural gift."

The Prince and the Showgirl (1957), *Some Like It Hot* (1959), *Let's Make Love* (1960), and *The Misfits* (1961). Of these, only *Some Like It Hot* was a huge success, and it remains one of the most celebrated examples of subtly queer-themed efforts of classical Hollywood.

Privately, Marilyn was noted for her liberal attitudes, which extended to members of the LGBTQ+ and other marginalized communities. At the time of her death in 1962, at the age of thirty-six, Marilyn was possibly the most widely adored queer icon of a generation, and her popularity would endure for decades to come. To the pre-Stonewall queers, she symbolized the struggle for acceptance, visibility, and respect. To those who came after, she became a cultural martyr, a woman who stood in direct contrast with the era of conformity and prejudice in which she existed, and who, despite her tragic demise, emerged somehow victorious—an icon for the ages.

ELIZABETH
TAYLOR

Elizabeth Taylor is something of a mother figure for the queer community. As far back as the early 1950s, while still in her teens, Taylor started befriending Hollywood's tortured and closeted gays, counting Montgomery Clift, James Dean, Roddy McDowall, and Rock Hudson among her dearest friends. Her love was unconditional, her support unwavering. In later years, long after the heyday of her legendary acting career, she continued to protect and speak out for the LGBTQ+ community, becoming the first high-profile celebrity to advocate on the behalf of AIDS victims, fighting the stigmatization and marginalization the community faced alongside the threat of the disease itself. Today, more than a decade after her death, Elizabeth Taylor remains a beloved icon and a true example of a staunch ally.

66 **A**ll of my life I've spent a lot of time with gay men—Montgomery Clift, Jimmy Dean, Rock Hudson—who were my colleagues, coworkers, confidantes, my closest friends, but I never thought of who they slept with. They were just the people I loved. I could never understand why they couldn't be afforded the same rights and protections as all of the rest of us." Elizabeth Taylor said these moving words during her speech at the 2000 GLAAD Awards. By then, she had already been recognized as one of the most celebrated champions of LGBTQ+ rights, as well as a fierce HIV/AIDS advocate. In the depth of the 1980s, when the US government was turning a blind eye to the mounting death toll and growing public hysteria surrounding AIDS, Taylor had taken a significant public stance, advocating for compassion for the stigmatized queer community and for vital research funding. And she didn't just advocate: a foundation she established in her own name raised millions, and it continues to be one of the leading organizations in the ongoing fight against HIV/AIDS.

Elizabeth Taylor knew that her name would carry enough weight to open doors, to get people to listen to what she had to say. After all, she had worked at establishing that name since the age of nine. Taylor grew up in front of the cameras, and by twelve she was a bona fide star. But while she represented the perfect image of a wholesome teenager to movie audiences, in reality she had little time to enjoy her formative years. It was this shared lack of a true childhood that would later serve as a basis for her close friendship with Michael Jackson.

With her role in *A Place in the Sun* (1951), Taylor played her first adult role, and it was also the first time she acted opposite Montgomery Clift, who became one of her closest friends. They'd make two more films together: *Raintree County* (1957) and *Suddenly, Last Summer* (1959), both of which brought Taylor Oscar nominations for Best Actress. Throughout the 1950s, Taylor's career progressed steadily, and by the middle of the decade she was one of the biggest stars in the industry. In 1955 she appeared opposite Rock Hudson and James Dean in *Giant*. The movie was a huge success and is today best remembered as Dean's last screen appearance before his tragic death. Elizabeth became close with Dean and was devastated by his death. She also formed a friendship with Rock Hudson, whose death from AIDS three decades later would prompt her to establish the Elizabeth Taylor Foundation. For the rest of the 1950s, she continued to appear in successful and often controversial films, including adaptations of two Tennessee Williams plays: *Cat on a Hot Tin Roof* (1958) and the aforementioned *Suddenly, Last Summer*. Both films tackled themes of homosexuality, and while the restrictions imposed by the Production Code made it impossible to bring the full force of Williams's original intent to the screen, for queer audiences in particular it wasn't difficult to see beyond the censorship.

By the time Elizabeth won her first Oscar, for *Butterfield 8* in 1960, she was widely regarded as the biggest movie star in the world, rivaled only by Marilyn Monroe. Her celebrity was due in no small part to her turbulent and often scandalous personal life: by the age of thirty, she had married four times, and while making *Cleopatra* in Rome (the role famously made her the first actor in history to be paid a million dollars for a single movie), she began a stormy affair with her costar, Richard Burton. Both were married at the time, and the liaison caused international outrage, even prompting the Vatican to denounce the couple. The scandal did little to diminish Taylor's popularity, and for the rest of the 1960s she and Burton, whom she married in 1964, symbolized the very pinnacle of fame and excess. Elizabeth's taste for liquor and expensive jewelry made headlines more often than her acting achievements, although in 1966 she did give the most acclaimed performance of her career, as Martha in *Who's Afraid of Virginia Woolf?*, which brought her a second Oscar for Best Actress.

The Burtons married and divorced twice, blazing through the popular culture landscape as one of the most dazzling celebrity couples of the past century. Despite their

"You cannot have passion of any kind unless you have compassion."

ultimate split, Taylor would maintain for the rest of her life that Burton, who died in 1976, was one of her two big loves (the other being producer Mike Todd, her third husband, who was tragically killed in a plane crash in 1958). She would go on to marry twice more, bringing the total to seven husbands and eight marriages. Later she joked that "those against gay marriage say that a marriage should only be between a man and a woman: my God, I of all people know that that doesn't always work!"

By the 1980s, when her acting career had all but finished, Taylor was considered a global icon whose status no longer depended on her movie roles. She was also a firmly established queer icon, celebrated for her glamour and campy excess as well as her wit and frankness. But it was her conduct and fierce advocacy in the face of the HIV pandemic that elevated her to the realm of queer icon supreme. Elizabeth Taylor raised the bar high for future icons: she demonstrated that it wasn't enough to be venerated by the community for her screen persona. She gave a piece of her true self to the LGBTQ+ community, significantly contributing to the shift of public attitudes toward those living with AIDS and to the entire queer tribe.

"There is no gay agenda, it's a human agenda," she told the GLAAD audience in 2000. "Why shouldn't gay people be able to live as open and freely as everybody else? What it comes down to, ultimately, is love. How can anything bad come out of love? The bad stuff comes out of mistrust, misunderstanding, and God knows, from hate, and from ignorance."

JAMES
DEAN

One of the original rebels of popular culture, James Dean redefined the notion of masculinity in American cinema. His unique blend of toughness and vulnerability, as well as the ambiguous sexuality he exuded on-screen, made him an instant queer icon, and one that has endured through the decades. Anyone who has ever felt misunderstood or alienated by the norms of patriarchy can relate to Dean as a universal symbol of freedom and defiance. Although Dean starred in only three films, two of which were released after his tragic death, he remains one of the most popular movie stars of all time, as well as one of the most beloved figures in all of LGBTQ+ iconography.

James Dean, alongside Montgomery Clift, Marlon Brando, and Sal Mineo, arrived on American movie screens in the early 1950s, shattering the established image of manhood. Perhaps more than any of his contemporaries, he came to embody the figure of the lone rebel, misunderstood by the establishment, lost in a postwar world of conservative values and very narrow views of human sexuality. Although Jimmy Dean's own sexuality was rarely the subject of public discourse until well after his death, queer audiences of the 1950s immediately recognized some of their own struggles in Jimmy's tortured screen persona. With his premature death at the age of twenty-four, Dean entered immortality, forever frozen into iconography as the rebellious teen of his celluloid incarnations.

Perhaps his most enduring legacy, both as an actor and a queer icon, remains his performance in *Rebel Without a Cause* (1955). The film threw traditional notions of masculinity into question, arguably for the first time in a mainstream movie, and established Dean as the leading figure in a growing movement of discontented teenagers and young adults, a generation that would, over the course of the next two decades, go on to reshape the cultural and political landscape of America. To those in the queer community, particularly to gay men, it was the relationship between James Dean and Sal Mineo that formed the heart of the movie. While strict rules of censorship prevented the filmmakers from explicitly stating that either of the characters was gay, the way the two actors played their parts left queer viewers with little doubt that what they were witnessing was a fully fledged same-sex love affair playing out before their eyes in a major Hollywood motion picture.

Rebel Without a Cause was released a month after Dean's death, and the film's success was steeped in widespread public grief, contributing to the cult following that grew around both actor and film.

Today, more than half a century later, the James Dean/Sal Mineo pairing in *Rebel* is still seen as one of the most prominent instances of queer representation ever included in a movie of the classical Hollywood period. More importantly, Dean himself remains an emblematic figure in the community, often employed as a symbol of queer power and resistance.

Born in a small town in Indiana, Dean spent his early childhood in California, before his beloved mother died of cancer when he was nine—a loss which would haunt him for the rest of his short life. His relationship with his father was strained, no doubt contributing to his later rebellion. Dean spent his teenage years raised by his aunt and uncle at a farm back in his home state. Fascinated by acting from an early age, the young and strikingly handsome Dean moved to California in 1949, hoping to study drama and make it in the film business. He quickly got work in television but struggled to break into movies, and he would often supplement his income with odd jobs, including as a parking lot attendant at CBS Studios. Discouraged by the lack of success in Hollywood, he moved to New York in 1951, where he quickly won a number of important stage roles and was admitted to the renowned Actors Studio, where he studied alongside Brando.

His breakthrough in movies came in 1953 when Elia Kazan cast him as Cal Trask in *East of Eden*. Dean's powerful performance was seen as a departure from the more traditional styles of screen acting, and he was hailed as one of the brightest talents of his generation. *East of Eden* made Dean an instant star, and he was cast in *Rebel Without a Cause*, directed by Nicholas Ray. It was Jimmy's idea to emphasize the homosexual aspect of the relationship between his character, Jim Stark, and Plato, played by Sal Mineo. Ray feared that the censors would object, but in the end even the National League of Decency failed to spot the rather obvious queer overtones, rating the film "unobjectionable." For an entire generation of queer boys and men, the film came to symbolize hope and at least a faint hint of visibility in an otherwise barren cultural landscape. *Giant*, Dean's last film, would see him playing Jett Rink, a ranch hand and drifter who becomes an oil millionaire. The movie's cast also included Elizabeth Taylor, who became a close friend of Dean in the last months of his life.

Dean's tragic death in a car accident, just weeks after shooting on *Giant* wrapped, sent shock waves around the world. Millions of

"Only the gentle are ever really strong."

teenagers mourned him as their hero but also as one of them. His death itself contributed to the romantic aura that still surrounds him—speeding along in his sports car, facing eternity head-on, the ultimate icon of freedom. To queer folk, however, he was all that and more. A decade after his death, Dean entered the pantheon of gay iconography when his image began to be claimed by the gay liberation movement. His status as a queer hero was further enhanced when biographies of the actor published in the 1970s hinted at his sexual orientation being other than straight. The ambiguous nature of his personal life, with various people claiming he was either bisexual or gay, only added to Dean's continuing appeal among the LGBTQ+ community. Today, he still appears ultramodern in his queerness—misunderstood in life, repressed by the constraints of his time, never allowed to fully embrace or express his true essence. The very fact that we celebrate him as an LGBTQ+ icon affords Dean at least some of the personal freedom he chased, but never attained, in life.

MONTGOMERY CLIFT

Deeply misunderstood and often portrayed as a victim of his own sexuality, Monty Clift was much more than the tragic figure he came to be known as. Seen as one of the most beautiful faces ever to grace the silver screen, Clift was a highly talented artist, credited for introducing Method acting to American cinema even before Brando and Dean. Renowned for portraying vulnerable, sensitive, and emotionally tortured characters, he is often seen as one of the leading male stars who redefined the image of cinematic masculinity. Since his untimely death, details of his personal life often dimmed his acting accomplishments, but it is his status as a queer icon that is perhaps his most enduring legacy.

Monty Clift was perhaps the first of the young, beautiful, and rebellious young men who burst onto movie screens in the years following the Second World War. He brought along a different sensibility and a multilayered, emotionally versatile persona that stood in direct contrast to the he-men of the preceding decades. He was also smart enough to realize that what he had to offer was different and made him a valuable commodity. He had known this before he ever made his movie debut.

While a successful stage actor in New York, Clift repeatedly rejected offers to sign a long-term contract with a movie studio, refusing to give up his independence and waiting for the right project to come to him. The opportunity came in 1947 with the script for *Red River*. In the movie, Clift portrayed a young and sensitive cowboy opposite John Wayne's worn-out, stereotypical macho character. The result of the pairing was exactly what Monty anticipated: the contrast between Clift's ultramodern, complex performance and Wayne's old-fashioned style catapulted the young actor to instant stardom. The movie also included the now-iconic scene in which Monty and John Ireland compare their guns—perhaps one of the most subtly homoerotic moments ever captured in a classic Western, and one so skillfully written that the censors missed the innuendo. It wasn't lost on queer audiences, however, who instantly noticed the devastatingly handsome Clift, and although details of his sexuality would not emerge for decades, he nonetheless became a gay icon at the very outset of his career.

Famously choosy about the parts he took and totally dedicated to his craft, Clift was seen as one of the most respected actors in the business, as well as one of the most bankable movie stars. The camera often focused on his beauty, and the narrative structures of his films made him into an object of female desire. This kind of visual adulation had previously been reserved for female stars, but Clift broke the mold. In films such as *The Search* (1948), *A Place in the Sun* (1951), *I Confess* (1953), and *From Here to Eternity* (1953), Clift's beauty was on full display, on par with his versatility as an actor. During the making of *A Place in the Sun*, Monty struck up a close friendship with his costar, Elizabeth Taylor, a relationship that was to last for the rest of his life. Taylor adored him, and Clift was able to confide his secrets to her. Monty's homosexuality was top-secret, and contrary to what some people suggested in the years following his death, Clift himself was comfortable with his preference for men. Far from the tortured, self-loathing figure portrayed in countless biographies and documentaries, intimate accounts released by his family in the 2018 film *Making Montgomery Clift* reveal a man of humor and sharp intelligence, confident and comfortable with his sexuality.

In 1957, while shooting the film *Raintree County* opposite Taylor, Clift sustained serious injuries in a car accident, which left his face almost completely crushed. He survived, but the physical pain caused by his injuries and the permanent change in his signature good looks altered his life forever. While some have referred to the remaining years of his life as "the longest suicide in Hollywood history," as Clift succumbed to addiction to drugs and alcohol, the truth is more complex. While certainly suffering pain and confronting his demons, Clift did not show any signs of suicidal behavior, and intimate tapes of his private conversations from the period reveal a man proud of his work and anticipating the future. In fact, the performances Clift gave after the accident are among his finest, including in *The Young Lions* (1958); *Suddenly, Last Summer* (1958), once again with Elizabeth Taylor; *The Misfits* (1961), in which he starred opposite Marilyn Monroe; *Judgment at Nuremberg* (1961); and *Freud: The Secret Passion* (1962).

Clift died in 1966 at the New York house he shared with his companion, Lorenzo James. James, fearing a homophobic and racist backlash, kept their relationship quiet, and in the following decades he rarely agreed to talk about Monty. Clift's death at the age of forty-five was seen as a tragic

"The sadness of our existence should not leave us blunted. On the contrary–how to remain thin-skinned, vulnerable, and stay alive?"

end to a sad life—a notion reinforced a decade later with the publication of a salacious biography, which detailed his struggles with sexuality, addictions, and the troubled relationship with his overbearing mother. This flawed account, however, actually helped establish Monty as a timeless queer icon, a man who was, above all, a victim of the time he lived in, unable to fully embrace who he was and the relationships he longed to establish. But besides the sadness, there is also the impressive legacy of a talented artist who left behind a body of work that stands the test of time. Searching for the real Monty Clift may still prove challenging, but perhaps it is in the work he so loved that we may find the most reliable clues.

MARLON BRANDO

His groundbreaking performance as Stanley Kowalski in *A Streetcar Named Desire* changed the course of screen acting. With his ultramasculine beauty, Brando at once represented brutality and tender vulnerability, but above all, his magnetic presence emanated irresistible sex appeal. His early roles established him firmly as a queer icon, and he was one of the first Hollywood celebrities to be open about his bisexuality. In *The Wild One*, he pioneered the leather biker look which was to become a staple among gay men, and he is also a noted lesbian icon. But far from being just eye candy, Brando was a true original—one of the most talented actors of the twentieth century as well as a fierce activist dedicated to fighting for the rights of others.

Marlon Brando burst on the scene with a raw, primal sexuality no one had seen in cinema before. With his appearance in 1951's screen adaptation of Tennessee Williams's Pulitzer Prize–winning play *A Streetcar Named Desire*, he single-handedly redefined the art of movie acting and established a new style that was to be emulated for decades to come. His strong, muscular body was put on full display, and in the same way Marilyn Monroe would become the new standard of fetishized feminine beauty, Brando was employed as an object of desire for female audiences. But despite his roughness, he also projected a sensitivity that cut through what would otherwise have been a one-dimensional persona, and it was this mix of contradicting qualities that made Brando such an intoxicating figure.

From the onset of his career, Brando attracted a queer following. His arresting gaze, perfect features, and hunky frame turned him into an instant poster boy for gay men, but it was his complex persona and independent, rebellious attitude toward the conservative society of the 1950s that made him the perfect icon of the fledgling gay liberation movement.

Like many other icons featured in this book, Brando's childhood was unstable and filled with conflict. The troubled teenager found it difficult to fit in at school, eventually being expelled for riding a motorcycle through the hallways. He transferred to a military school but dropped out before graduation and headed for New York City, where he finally found his place in the world of acting. From the start, it was clear that the young Brando had something special, and although he quickly acquired a reputation for being moody and uncooperative, his talent was undeniable. He was taken under the wing of the renowned acting teacher Stella Adler, whose influence would be profound. It was through Adler that he discovered the power of the Method, and he began studying at the Actors Studio.

His big break came in 1947 when he was cast in the original Broadway production of *A Streetcar Named Desire*, a monumental hit with both audiences and critics, with Brando's performance in particular gaining attention. Hailed as the next big star, he was cast in the film version, opposite Vivien Leigh. The movie was seen as revolutionary, and Brando, with his bulging biceps and tight undershirt, mumbling his lines in a way no actor had ever dared before, became an instant sex symbol and icon of cool. While he insisted he was nothing like Stanley (and in private detested the brutish character, who reminded him of his father), to the adoring public the actor and the part were hard to tell apart.

Other acclaimed performances quickly followed, including *Viva Zapata* (1952), *Julius Caesar* (1953), and *The Wild One* (1953), the last of which confirmed Brando's status as queer icon. His image as the leather-wearing leader of a motorcycle gang looked like an iconic Tom of Finland illustration come to life, and he became an idol for an entire segment of the community. To gay men who looked for a sense of belonging, the pioneering gay motorcycle and leather clubs were a rare opportunity to find like-minded individuals. At the same time

Brando, along with James Dean, also became an early icon for the lesbian community, for whom he represented rebellion and butch sensibility at odds with traditional norms imposed by society.

In 1955 Brando won his first Best Actor Oscar for his performance in *On the Waterfront,* and for the remainder of the decade he continued to be seen as a top box-office star. Always outspoken and resentful of the hypocrisy he witnessed in Hollywood, Brando was one of the most elusive of movie stars. By the 1960s his career slowed down considerably, and the majority of his films in this period were seen as disappointments. Perhaps the most notable entry in his filmography from this decade is *Reflections in a Golden Eye* (1967), in which he plays a closeted army officer married to Elizabeth Taylor. His willingness to play a gay character at a time when most of his fellow A-listers still shied away from it points to Brando's disregard for Hollywood's petty politics and his attitude toward social prejudice. During the sixties he was heavily involved in the fight for civil rights, taking part in the March on Washington in 1963. He was also famously a supporter of Native American causes. When he received his second Academy Award, for his great comeback performance in *The Godfather* (1972), Sacheen Littlefeather, a Native American woman, appeared onstage on his behalf and informed the audience that Brando

"If we are not our brother's keeper, at least let us not be his executioner."

would not accept his award due to the poor treatment of Native Americans by the film industry.

Brando's personal life was chaotic and legendary for his countless love affairs with both men and women. He married three times and fathered eleven children, and his many liaisons were rumored to have included James Dean, Montgomery Clift, and Marilyn Monroe. One of the most meaningful and long-lasting relationships of Brando's life was his deeply intimate friendship with the actor Wally Cox. The two had met while still at school, where Brando played savior to the shy and bullied Cox. Their relationship lasted until Cox's death in 1973, and after Brando's death in 2004, in accordance with his wishes, their ashes were mixed together and scattered in Death Valley.

In 1976 Brando told a journalist, "Like a large number of men I too have had homosexual experiences, and I am not ashamed. I have never paid much attention to what people think of me." His independent spirit never left him, and he remained a reclusive, enigmatic figure until the end. Later in his career he could still turn in magnificent performances, as he did in *Last Tango in Paris* (1972), *The Missouri Breaks* (1976), and *Apocalypse Now* (1979). His final years were marred by ill health and personal tragedy, but he never stopped being an iconic and highly respected, if at times controversial, figure.

Brando's legacy as one of the greatest actors of our time is firmly secured. So is his status as one of the original rebels, a symbol of cool and nonconformity, and an enduring icon of the LGBTQ+ community.

SAL
MINEO

Sal Mineo's unforgettable performance as the closeted gay teenager in love with James Dean's character in *Rebel Without a Cause* is part of our collective queer consciousness. At a time when any hint of homosexuality, both on-screen and in real life, was seen as deviant, Mineo introduced a new kind of gay character: sensitive, complex, sympathetic, even heroic—in many ways the actual rebel of the film's title. But the real Sal Mineo had plenty of causes for rebellion: as one of the first Hollywood actors to openly discuss his queerness, he became an icon even before his tragic, mysterious death, his brutal murder continuing to serve as a symbol of queer martyrdom.

Like his *Rebel Without a Cause* costars James Dean and Natalie Wood, Sal Mineo met a tragic and premature end, but unlike them, he is today largely forgotten by the mainstream. Outside of the LGBTQ+ community, where Mineo's legacy as one of the trailblazers who brought queer identity to the American screen lives on, his work lies neglected in the shadow of his more iconic contemporaries: Dean, Brando, Newman, and Clift. But to reexamine his work and his personal contribution to queer culture is to find a multifaceted, versatile actor and a brave visionary who was among the first in Hollywood not only to speak openly about his sexual orientation but also to incorporate his queer identity into his work.

Born in the Bronx to Sicilian immigrant parents, Mineo would find that his ethnic background was as much of an obstacle in Hollywood as his sexuality. Blessed with striking beauty and natural talent, he quickly moved up the ranks of television, where he established himself as a successful young actor. But his role as the shy, closeted teen Plato in *Rebel Without a Cause* altered his fate forever. Mineo played the part so well that for the remainder of his life people would fail to distinguish between the actor and the part he created. The film's narrative, while unquestionably progressive in its representation of queerness, nevertheless reflected the attitudes of the period. While Plato was allowed to fall in love with James Dean's character, and even have his love somewhat requited, albeit covertly, he still had to pay for his homosexuality by dying a violent death at the end of the movie. The fact that Mineo himself would one day meet an eerily similar fate only adds to the poignancy of the role he has played as a quintessential gay icon of his time.

Rebel Without a Cause was naturally not seen as a queer film at the time of its release. In fact, even one of the film's screenwriters,

Stewart Stern, later admitted being only partially aware of the significance the relationship between Dean and Mineo had for the gay audience. The effect on those who saw the film in the darkness of America's movie theaters was profound: the image of Mineo, with the picture of Alan Ladd in his locker, gazing longingly and lovingly at Dean was perhaps the first chance any queer people had to witness a glimpse of their own desires represented on-screen. While the mainstream cast Mineo as yet another addition to the growing number of teenage idols of the 1950s, promoting his image of the very much straight heartthrob, to queer cinemagoers he would remain a symbol of their own closeted struggle.

His youthful good looks carried Mineo through the rest of the 1950s, though he continued to be cast as a copy of Plato, never quite achieving leading-man status. He recorded pop songs and scored his second Oscar nomination for the 1960s drama *Exodus* (his first had been for *Rebel Without a Cause*). Despite his success, by the start of the sixties he was considered played out in Hollywood, and he would struggle to find steady employment for the rest of his life. This was partly due to the rumors that surrounded his personal life—while he maintained relationships with women, it was common knowledge that he had gay lovers. By the 1970s Mineo talked openly about his sexuality, and about the fact that Hollywood was full of closeted homosexuals who were unable to come out due to the industry's prejudice. His frankness did little to further his crumbling career in movies, but by then Mineo had turned his creative energy toward the stage. In 1969 he directed and starred in the controversial, queer-themed *Fortune and Men's Eyes*, which tackled the subject of homophobia and abuse in the American prison system.

While Mineo's career never reached the heights he enjoyed after *Rebel*, he never lost hope that he would find success again. He was well loved in the theater community, and the growing gay liberation movement held his pioneering efforts as a queer creative in high esteem. At the time of his murder, Mineo had been rehearsing for a new play alongside his boyfriend of six years, Courtney Burr. His death sent shock waves through Hollywood but even more profoundly through the gay community, which saw it as a clear manifestation of the violence and prejudice they faced. Even if the criminal investigation eventually established that Mineo's death wasn't motivated by homophobia, with the clear cause and exact circumstances never fully explained, in the popular belief the tragedy continues to serve as an example of queer martyrdom.

But beyond his tragic death, Sal Mineo's legacy shines brighter than ever. It is the legacy of a queer star, so rare in his era, who overcame the limitations of his time to become a queer icon for the generations who came after.

"We were all very young and we played young people —all of a sudden, the revolution started."

TAB
HUNTER

In the 1950s, few names conjured up more excitement than Tab Hunter's. With his magnetic screen presence and picture-perfect good looks, he amassed legions of devoted fans, mostly young girls who'd swoon at the very mention of his name. To gay cinemagoers, he was the embodiment of a perfect homoerotic fantasy. While fan magazines tried to pair him up with gorgeous female stars, from Natalie Wood to Debbie Reynolds, few outside his close circle knew that the most eligible bachelor in Hollywood was in fact gay. It was a secret that Tab Hunter would carry for more than half a century, finally revealing the truth in his 2005 autobiography.

In the years following the end of the Second World War, America was determined to regain its balance and sense of control. All-American, wholesome images of robust beauty were in high demand, and Hollywood studios delivered the goods. Tab Hunter was in many ways the quintessential figure of his time, a teen idol and poster boy for a new, more optimistic, and prosperous time. But like the era he came to embody, there was a darker side to his story.

Abandoned by an abusive father, Tab spent most of his childhood in California, attending Catholic schools, singing in church choirs, and figure skating. His German mother was devoutly religious, and the rigid teachings of the church instilled in the young boy a deep sense of shame and guilt he would carry with him for many years. Homosexuality was seen as sinful if it was mentioned at all, and as Tab would remember decades later, being openly gay wasn't an option. While it was apparent early on that he was in possession of extraordinary good looks, the attention he frequently received from his female peers only made him more embarrassed and uncomfortable.

Acting was not something he ever dreamed of, and yet screen stardom seemed an inevitable fate for the strikingly handsome young drifter. Spotted by the Hollywood agent Henry Willson, who famously specialized in discovering young and attractive male stars, the newly renamed Tab Hunter quickly became successful, even if his early roles were panned by critics. While many of his most famous contemporaries, such as Montgomery Clift, James Dean, and Marlon Brando, were implementing the famed Method and bringing raw realism to screen acting, Tab represented the safer, more wholesome side of the 1950s. He became one of the most popular stars of the decade, particularly appealing to teenage girls, who saw him as the perfect embodiment of a dreamboat. Their mothers were prone to agree: while rebels such as Dean or Brando were seen as a bad influence, Tab Hunter was the kind of boy every mother wanted her daughter to bring home.

Tab's success grew, with better film roles and more established costars as well as a recording career. It's been said that Jack Warner founded Warner Records in order to keep tabs on the young star's unexpected chart success. Hunter established himself as one of the most bankable young actors after appearing in 1955's *Battle Cry*. What followed was a string of popular films that paired him with stars such as Natalie Wood, further enhancing his image as a major leading man. For the sake of publicity, Warner Bros. promoted Hunter and Wood as a romantic couple offscreen as well. The studio arranged other dates for their star, including with actress Debbie Reynolds. Although Tab would form close friendships with both Wood and Reynolds, his true romantic escapades were kept secret.

In the Hollywood of the 1950s, any hint of a homosexual scandal was guaranteed to destroy even the most established career, and Tab, along with many of Henry Willson's other clients, including Rock Hudson, took every precaution to keep his sexuality hidden from the world. As Tab would later remark, Hollywood is a place where "you are rewarded for being something you are not." Leading a double life was hard and often traumatizing, and in that respect Tab's own hardships mirrored those faced by his queer audience. With his reputation as a favorite among female cinemagoers firmly established and heavily promoted, what Hunter was perhaps unaware of at the time was his significant gay following. Across America, in small-town theaters and at drive-ins, young, closeted gay men gazed longingly at the larger-than-life image of Tab Hunter projected on the screen. Few could have imagined that Hollywood's number-one symbol of masculinity was part of their own tribe.

In private, Hunter explored his sexuality through a series of clandestine romances, perhaps the most significant of which was his long-term relationship with Anthony Perkins. The two would often go out on "double dates," taking out a couple of female friends for the sake of appearance. While today they would no doubt be considered a major power couple, and a very attractive one at that, at the time, if discovered, their love would have meant a kiss of death to both their careers. In the end, the pressures of remaining in the closet became too great, and the relationship ended in 1959, a year before Perkins achieved international stardom in Alfred Hitchcock's *Psycho*.

The painful loss of Perkins signaled the beginning of the end of Tab's stardom. As the 1950s closed, his bright, all-American

"In my personal life, I was quite a different Boy Next Door than the one Mr. and Mrs. Middle America pictured me to be."

image fell out of favor with audiences who were now looking for different kinds of idols. With the decline of the studio system, Tab Hunter became a relic of an epoch that was becoming increasingly unpopular among younger audiences, and by the mid-1960s he had left Hollywood. His career would experience a period of resurgence in the 1980s, when underground director John Waters offered him a part in his low-budget film *Polyester* opposite Divine. The unlikely pairing of a handsome Hollywood leading man and a larger-than-life drag queen was a surprise sensation, launching Waters and Divine into mainstream success and providing Tab with a new generation of fans. He would later star in another successful Divine comedy, *Lust in the Dust*. The film's producer, Allan Glaser, became Tab's longtime partner, and he encouraged Hunter to embrace both his sexual identity and his queer following.

After more than half a century of speculation, Tab Hunter officially came out of the closet in 2005 with the publication of his autobiography, *Tab Hunter Confidential: The Making of a Movie Star*. The book was an important milestone in the history of queer Hollywood: Hunter was the only major star from the 1950s who lived to tell his story, to embrace his sexuality and his true identity, and to shed light on the hardships of being gay in a stiflingly homophobic time and industry. And while his image belongs to a bygone era, his struggles as a gay film star feel disturbingly current. A year before his death, Hunter reflected: "Film actors today still fear that coming out would damage their career." It is possible that while Tab Hunter spent the majority of his life and career in the closet, the brave decision to come out at the end of his life may prove to be his most enduringly precious legacy.

TENNESSEE WILLIAMS

Considered one of the greatest American writers of the twentieth century, Tennessee Williams created an enchanted world, populated with flamboyant characters and poetic language, and introduced the very aesthetics of queerness to literary and popular culture. His plays and their movie adaptations offered queer audiences a reality in which they no longer felt alone or invisible. His characters were often drunks and losers, hopeless dreamers and faded beauty queens—people victimized by society and by their own desires. Williams's greatest plays, such as *A Streetcar Named Desire* and *Cat on a Hot Tin Roof*, are considered inspired masterpieces, at once emblematic of the social realities of their time and universal in their unique insight into the human condition. While he rarely offered a happy, or even a hopeful, ending, Williams explored the dark corners of life, always with great artistry and without judgment.

Tennessee Williams is more than a gay icon; he created a world in which other gay icons could be born. Starting with the success of *The Glass Menagerie* in 1944, which introduced Williams's signature style of poetic realism, over the next two decades he created a number of masterpieces that became central to shaping the cultural identity of queerness. Williams was open about his sexuality throughout his career, but the restraints of the time prevented him from ever being able to write a fully fledged gay play. This didn't stop him from weaving queer narrative into everything he wrote, however. From disguising his own identity behind female characters to subtle yet decisive hints of queerness, Williams is one of the pioneers of LGBTQ+ literature. His 1947 play *A Streetcar Named Desire* is considered one of the greatest plays in the canon of American drama, and its legendary 1948 Broadway production starring Marlon Brando and directed by Elia Kazan is considered a milestone that forever changed American theater. Throughout the fifties and early sixties, film adaptations of Williams's works, though often sanitized for the screen by censorship, were nonetheless vehicles for queer stories and characters—from fragile Blanche in *A Streetcar Named Desire* (1951), portrayed by Vivien Leigh, who many consider to be Williams's literary self-portrait; to the more explicitly gay-themed *Cat on a Hot Tin Roof* (1958); to *Suddenly, Last Summer* (1959) and *The*

Roman Spring of Mrs. Stone (1961). Aside from portraying the difficulties of gay life in an era of prejudice and hypocrisy, Williams was also renowned for writing complex parts for women. Many of these helped the actresses who played them to achieve the gay icon status they still enjoy today, from Vivien Leigh to Elizabeth Taylor, who both starred in multiple Williams adaptations.

Born to a religious Southern family, Williams's childhood would be a source of both inspiration and trauma for the rest of his life. Many of his most iconic characters were derived from his closest family—his mother, Edwina; his sister, Rose; and his volatile, sometimes violent father, Cornelius. Rose would be later diagnosed with schizophrenia, and the shadow of her mental illness lingers over most of Tennessee's work. While he initially tried to date women, mostly to appease his traditionalist parents, by the 1940s he was living as a gay man. And although homosexuality was considered a mental illness as well as a criminal act, Williams chose to live fairly openly for his time. His various romantic relationships and sexual adventures also found their way into his plays, though often the figure of the gay man was disguised by a female character.

Williams's first big success came in 1944 with *The Glass Menagerie*. It was a thinly veiled representation of Williams's relationship with his mother and sister, with Tom (Williams's given name) as the unhappy and repressed gay son. The play became a huge hit and made Williams a literary celebrity overnight. The follow-up to *Menagerie* would turn out to be an even bigger success, winning Williams the Pulitzer Prize and a place among the most celebrated dramatists of the century. *A Streetcar Named Desire* opened on Broadway in 1947, causing a sensation. The production dealt with themes of homosexuality, repressed desire, prostitution, and rape—all of which were considered taboo at the time. The play also catapulted its lead actor, Marlon Brando, to instant stardom. When it came to casting the movie version, there was no doubt that Brando would reprise his role, while Vivien Leigh, who starred in the London production, was brought in to play Blanche. The film, while slightly toned down to appease the censors, still packed a heavy punch, revolutionizing the art of screen acting and introducing new and daring themes to mainstream cinema.

Tennessee Williams would continue his exploration of themes relating to homosexuality and its treatment by society in other plays during the 1950s, most notably in *Cat on a Hot Tin Roof*, which won him a second Pulitzer Prize, and *Suddenly, Last Summer*. Both plays were adapted as Hollywood movies, and both starred Elizabeth Taylor. While conservative critics

"What is straight? A line can be straight, or a street, but the human heart, oh, no, it's curved like a road through mountains."

scorned them, audiences flocked to see the movies. For many, including queer viewers, seeing a Tennessee Williams play or movie was the first time they came face to face with homosexual narratives and characters. These stories themselves rarely offered a hopeful ending—being taken to a mental asylum (*Streetcar*), eaten by cannibals (*Suddenly, Last Summer*), or resigning oneself to a straight relationship (*Cat on a Hot Tin Roof*) were just some of the endings Williams envisaged for his characters. And yet the fate written for his protagonists seemed more a reflection of the social attitudes of the time than his own view of queerness.

In his personal life, Williams maintained a long-term relationship with actor Frank Merlo, which lasted on and off till Merlo's death in 1963. Plagued by depression and drug addiction, Williams struggled to maintain his successful string, with *The Night of the Iguana* and its subsequent 1964 film adaptation considered to be his last big success. Although he never stopped writing, the last two decades of his life were filled with personal struggle and professional disappointment.

In the decades following his death, Williams continued to mesmerize new generations of theatergoers with his timeless, lyrical plays and unforgettable characters. His legacy as an important storyteller and a voice for the queer community during a time in history when visibility was practically nonexistent remains as alive as ever.

BARBRA STREISAND

Barbra's meteoric rise to stardom during the 1960s coincided with the growing unrest in the LGBTQ+ community. With her unconventional style, powerful screen presence, and once-in-a-generation voice, she became the first ultramodern queer icon, perfectly suited for the Stonewall era. She had begun her career by performing in the Greenwich Village gay bars, and by the time she hit the mainstream, Streisand already had a steadfast queer following, which only grew as the years went on. Six decades of hit records and iconic movie characters later, Barbra Streisand is still a quintessential icon, representing a blueprint for the pop songstresses who followed in her footsteps.

Growing up in Brooklyn during the 1940s and '50s, young Barbra loved the movies, which offered an escape from her own troubled life. From an early age her ambition was to act, though it was hard for her to see herself represented among the leading ladies of classical Hollywood. Streisand knew she was different, and her insecurity was further deepened by her mother's assessment, according to which she simply wasn't beautiful enough to ever make it as an actress. From the beginning, though, it was clear that one thing Barbra could do was sing. Her voice would be her ticket out, and by the age of twenty, she had already established herself as a star of the New York nightclub scene and a Tony-nominated stage actress. She quickly followed her success with popular appearances on TV talk shows and her first album, *The Barbra Streisand Album*, which was released in 1963. The record made her a star and won her three Grammy awards.

By the end of the decade, Barbra Streisand was one of the biggest stars in the business, thanks to her Broadway success as Fanny Brice in *Funny Girl* in 1964. The musical introduced some of the numbers that would become Streisand's signature songs, including "People" and "Don't Rain on My Parade." The movie version, directed by the legendary William Wyler, was released in 1968 and catapulted Barbra to instant movie stardom, winning her the Best Actress Oscar—tied that year with another queer icon, Katharine Hepburn.

By this point, Streisand's stage and screen personas were highly refined and her style instantly recognizable. There were elements of high camp, as well as her signature sense of humor, all of which assured her status as a queer icon. She became a favorite subject of drag impersonators, with many of her early songs earning a permanent spot in the LGBTQ+ catalog.

Barbra Streisand looked different and behaved differently from the classic movie star image, and yet she turned all of these differences to her own advantage. It was this defiance of the established standards of beauty and style that so endeared her to her queer fans: Streisand just didn't care, and from the start of her career she made her own standards.

Her star continued to rise throughout the 1970s, with more iconic movie appearances in *Hello, Dolly!* (1969); *The Owl and the Pussycat* (1970); *What's Up, Doc* (1971); *The Way We Were* (1973); and *A Star Is Born* (1976). Her films were hugely popular, and Streisand featured on the top 10 box office draws throughout the decade, many times as the sole female actor on the list. She also continued her phenomenal success as a recording artist, with such era-defining hits as "No More Tears (Enough Is Enough)," a duet with Donna Summer that would became another gay anthem; "The Way We Were"; and "Evergreen." After she forgot the lyrics to a couple of her songs during a concert in 1967, Streisand largely stayed away from performing live for the next two decades, but her absence had little impact on her album sales, which continued to break records. In 1980 she released *Guilty*, a pop album she recorded with Barry Gibb that

became an instant classic and once again a queer favorite, with the title song featuring the lyric "And we got nothing to be sorry of, our love is one in a million, eyes can see that we got a highway to the sky," often seen as an affirmation of gay love.

Throughout the decades, Barbra never stopped following her own artistic instincts, even when they went against industry wisdom, recording albums of Broadway tunes and jazz standards and helping to popularize both genres beyond their niches. She also applied the same determination to her movie career. In 1983 she made history by becoming the first woman to produce, direct, cowrite, and star in a major motion picture. *Yentl* was a labor of love that took more than a decade to come to fruition and remains a triumphant achievement of female-driven cinema. The musical drama tells the story of a young Jewish girl in early twentieth-century Poland who decides to pass herself off as a boy in order to obtain the education she craves but which is denied to women by her Orthodox community. The film's gender representation and blurred lines between male and female, with hints of queer desire, made *Yentl* an important LGBTQ+ classic, a status it still enjoys today.

Throughout the years, Streisand faced criticism for her single-mindedness and perfectionism, a criticism often rooted in sexism. She continued to defy stereotypes

"We are alike. We all want peace and happiness and family and love and understanding."

and break barriers, both as a filmmaker and a recording artist, directing such movies as *The Prince of Tides* (1991) and *The Mirror Has Two Faces* (1996). Among her unrealized projects is the film adaptation of Larry Kramer's play *The Normal Heart*, telling the story of the AIDS crisis through the eyes of an ensemble of gay characters. Streisand purchased the movie rights to the play after first seeing it in the 1980s, and although she never managed to bring it to the screen, in 1993 she did organize a special reading of the play to raise funds for AIDS-related causes.

Today, at eighty, Barbra Streisand is a living legend and one of the most beloved queer icons of all time. "The gay community supported me from the start and I will always be grateful," she wrote in a 2017 "Love Letter to the LGBTQ Community." "We're all unique and beautiful in our own way and entitled to love and be loved by whomever we choose."

LIZA MINNELLI

It seemed inevitable that the only daughter of Judy Garland and MGM director Vincente Minnelli would grow up to be a star in her own right. Liza Minnelli more than lived up to those expectations—she became a legend and one of the most celebrated queer icons of all time, rivaled perhaps only by her mother. Her name alone suggests stardom and glamour. In a career spanning more than six decades, Minnelli sang, acted, and danced her way into sequin-studded immortality, and she continues to be one of the most instantly recognizable figures in the pantheon of LGBTQ+ icons.

Few names are as synonymous with show business as that of Liza Minnelli. Equally few entertainers can even begin to compare to Liza's legendary status in the queer iconography. This is partly due to her heritage—being the daughter of the ultimate gay icon, Judy Garland, gave Liza a head start in building her own queer following. But fame by association will only take you so far, and since making her Broadway debut and winning her first Tony Award at the age of nineteen, Liza Minnelli has worked tirelessly to make a name for herself independent of her parents' achievements.

She made her first movie appearance in 1949, aged three, in *In the Good Old Summertime* opposite her mother. It was hardly a star-making role, but it signaled the beginning of a lifetime of performing. Liza grew up surrounded by the luminaries of Hollywood's golden age. To her they were simply the friends and colleagues of her parents.

Many of these figures were queer, the architects of the dream factory. Liza's early exposure to queer sensibilities, not least through the influence of her beloved father who was himself gay, would play an important role in shaping her star persona and her personal loyalty to the community, which she has shown throughout her life.

Determined to make it as a dancer and singer, Liza moved to New York while still in her teens. She found that her name would open many doors, but it was her talent that determined whether or not she'd be hired. She soon proved herself more than worthy of her legacy—from the start Liza possessed a star quality that made her impossible to overlook. Her mother saw her worth when she invited the then eighteen-year-old Liza to appear with her at a concert at the London Palladium. The now-iconic duet between the two clearly showed that, despite lack of experience, Liza was more than capable of holding her own opposite her legendary mother. While Garland's star dimmed, Liza's was on the rise. She recorded a number of popular albums and soon began appearing in motion pictures. It was instantly apparent that, much like her mother, Liza was not only a charismatic singer but could give a powerful dramatic performance. In 1969, the year of her mother's death, she delivered a highly acclaimed performance as the eccentric Pookie Adams in *The Sterile Cuckoo*, a role that brought her an Academy Award nomination for Best Actress.

She won the coveted award three years later for her iconic turn as Sally Bowles in Bob Fosse's musical masterpiece *Cabaret* (1972). The film was one of the first mainstream movies to show an openly bisexual character as well as a polyamorous sexual relationship. *Cabaret* has since entered the canon of cinematic classics, and Liza's brilliant performance is still considered one of cinema's finest. The film also helped to establish Liza's iconic look, which has been copied and lovingly impersonated by drag artists ever since. In the same year, Liza recorded a television concert, *Liza with a Z*, which earned her an Emmy Award and became another legendary event, instrumental in establishing Minnelli as one of the most dynamic performers of her, or any, generation.

Although she gave further acclaimed performances in movies such as *New York, New York* (1977), *Arthur* (1981), and *Stepping Out* (1991), Minnelli's cinematic output has been rather limited. Throughout her career she has thrived mainly as a live performer: her sold-out shows at Carnegie Hall, Radio City Music Hall, and the Olympia in Paris have entered showbiz mythology. Her razzle-dazzle style is an instant throwback to the golden era of Hollywood musicals and Las Vegas shows, but she has also demonstrated her versatility, recording pop and jazz albums as well. In 1989, she released *Results*, a dance-pop record produced by the Pet Shop Boys that became an instant LGBTQ+ classic. She is one of the handful of performers to hold the coveted EGOT—Emmy, Grammy, Oscar, and Tony Awards.

Her following in the community has endured and strengthened through the years, not only due to her larger-than-life, instantly recognizable brand of fabulousness but also because of the love and support she has given back to her queer fans. "Where would I be without the LGBTQ community of dazzling souls who have always supported and understood me on a level that is unique and extraordinary?" she wrote in 2017. Throughout the decades, some of Liza's closest friends have had strong ties to the queer community: from the fashion designer Halston to Rock Hudson and

"You learn to take other people's opinions less seriously. I think you just gotta go straight ahead and do what you want to do and do it well."

the Queen front man himself, Freddie Mercury. In 1994 Liza performed a touching tribute to AIDS victims at the twenty-fifth anniversary of the Stonewall riots, which erupted the night after her mother's funeral. She had been one of the earliest and most outspoken supporters of gay rights, as well as an advocate for the destigmatization of AIDS sufferers. Her intimate link to the com-

munity was confirmed when she made a cameo appearance in *Sex and the City 2* (2010), where she officiated a same-sex wedding—the ultimate gay fantasy.

Liza has always embraced her status, even before it became fashionable to do so. She is one of the great queer icons, the ones where only the first name is needed to instantly identify them. That's Liza. With a Z.

JAMES
BALDWIN

Considered one of the great literary voices of his generation, James Baldwin had to navigate his way through a hostile world, facing prejudice both as a gay man and as an African American. At the dawn of the civil rights and gay liberation movements, Baldwin captured the unique feeling present in both communities while also painting a broader picture of society as seen through the eyes of the marginalized. His various collections of essays, as well as his groundbreaking 1956 novel *Giovanni's Room*, continue to inspire new generations of readers, still constituting one of the finest examples of the queer perspective in all of literature.

James Baldwin is a unique figure, both in terms of his literary output and his activism. His experience as a Black queer man in America was one of rejection and disillusionment on multiple levels. In this he was certainly not alone, as Black LGBTQ+ individuals continue to face higher degrees of violence and prejudice, both within the African American community and from society at large. Baldwin's writing is an invaluable record of that experience at a particularly vital moment in history. For obvious reasons, Baldwin did not openly discuss his homosexuality before the 1970s, yet he had become an important voice for the cause of gay liberation as early as 1956, the year his controversial novel *Giovanni's Room* was published. Baldwin's sexuality was an open secret—especially as he never denied it—and his reputation as a "queer writer" would lead to discrimination from within his own community. While fully committed in his fight for racial equality and civil rights, Baldwin was de facto excluded from the inner circle of civil rights activists, as his sexual orientation was seen as harmful to the cause.

Born in Harlem to a single mother, Baldwin grew up unaware of the identity of his father. A sensitive child who struggled to blend in with his peers, he was drawn to literature and art from an early age. As a teenager, his emerging queer identity contributed to his feelings of otherness and isolation. Forced to help the family financially, Baldwin juggled his time between studying and working a string of manual jobs. He was an artist, but he found it hard to believe that he would ever make a living from his writing.

Growing up, he experienced both racism and homophobia, and by his early twenties he felt disillusioned and depressed, unable to find a place for himself in his own country. In 1948 he moved to Paris, where he would finally spread his literary wings. Here he was able to explore his own sexuality and come to terms with his queer identity. In Paris Baldwin also began tackling the subjects of homosexuality, homophobia, and toxic masculinity in his work, notably in his early essays *Preservation of Innocence* (1949) and *The Male Prison* (1954).

Baldwin's first novel was the highly autobiographical *Go Tell It on the Mountain* (1953), which was then followed by his most enduring works: a collection of essays entitled *Notes of a Native Son* (1955) and the queer novel *Giovanni's Room*.

Giovanni's Room remains an important milestone in the history of the queer novel. Published more than a decade before the Stonewall riots, it was a brave statement on homoerotic desire and queer shame as well as a meditation on the repressive social structures of the time. Literary critics still debate the fact that Baldwin chose to make his characters white; he later explained that he didn't think it was possible to deal with the issues of racism and the antagonism toward gay people in a single work. Despite this, the book was permeated with racial consciousness and a careful dissection of the bigotry of the 1950s. The novel was met with a great deal of controversy, particularly in the United States, but it was also

acclaimed by critics and positioned Baldwin among the most esteemed writers of his generation. He was able to use this platform for his civil rights activism, even if he was never fully admitted into the movement's ranks due to his homosexuality. While Baldwin took part in the March on Washington in 1963, making an appearance alongside his friends Marlon Brando and Sidney Poitier, he was excluded from making a speech.

While he continued to be one of the most prominent figures in the civil rights dialogue, he never saw himself as one of the mainstream activists, instead choosing to maintain an independent voice. He spent most of his later years living in France, where he continued to write essays, short stories, and novels, including the queer-themed short story *The Outing* (published in his 1965 collection *Going to Meet the Men*) and the novels *Tell Me How Long the Train's Been Gone* (1968) and *Just Above My Head* (1979). He became an iconic figure in the gay liberation movement, particularly for the African American and Latino communities, who had been marginalized by the mainstream faction of the movement. From the early 1970s, Baldwin became more explicit in voicing his support for queer issues, addressing America's homophobia in a number of public interviews and essays.

Baldwin died at his home in the south of France, where he had lived for many

"Not everything that is faced can be changed, but nothing can be changed until it is faced."

years. He left behind a rich and important legacy, as a writer and as a voice of wisdom and reason. His literary output transcends genres, as it does racial boundaries, and yet it is also unquestionably vital to both queer and Black history. Baldwin's image challenged the idea of traditional masculinity, especially in the context of what Black maleness meant. He was perhaps the first well-known African American to be openly queer, offering hope and visibility to those who had previously felt there was no place for them. While navigating the complex sociopolitical landscape of the time was certainly a difficult task, Baldwin managed to do so with grace and heroism, establishing himself as one of the most important LGBTQ+ icons of all time.

MARSHA P. JOHNSON

Considered the patron saint of the LGBTQ+ community, Marsha P. Johnson was a pioneering activist, a flamboyant Village queen, and an iconic figure in her own lifetime. On a hot June night in 1969, Marsha was among the street queens who fought back against police brutality for the first time, sparking the Stonewall riots and giving birth to the modern LGBTQ+ rights movement. Some say that it was Marsha "Pay It No Mind" Johnson who first threw a shot glass against a mirror, shouting, "I got my civil rights!" and giving birth to the legend of the "shot glass heard round the world."

Marsha P. Johnson represents the underdog, the marginalized within a marginalized group, who nonetheless carried the torch for the entire community, trailblazing and fighting, flowers in her hair. Marsha was Black, trans, often homeless, and destitute, and yet managed to become a legend. Known as the Mayor of Christopher Street, Johnson came to represent all those whose voices were often unheard or even purposely silenced, but who nonetheless constituted an indispensable pillar of the LGBTQ+ community. It is fair to say that all of us owe an enormous debt of gratitude to Marsha and other pioneering queens on the fringes of queerdom who put their own lives on the line for the betterment of all.

Born in New Jersey to Malcolm Michaels Sr. and Alberta (Claiborne) Michaels, little Marsha experienced sexual violence and prejudice early on. When she first started wearing girls' clothes at the age of five, she was raped by a thirteen-year-old boy, an experience that left lasting psychological trauma. At the age of seventeen, she moved to New York City with a suitcase of clothes and fifteen dollars in her pocket. She waited tables and soon turned to hustling on the streets of Greenwich Village. It was here that she earned her name—initially known as Black Marsha, she soon changed it to Marsha P. (for Pay It No Mind) Johnson after the Howard Johnson's restaurant on Forty-Second Street. Although broke and often sleeping on the streets, Marsha soon became a noted figure in the Village set, due mainly to her joyous, generous personality and ingenious ability to transform cheap items of clothing into striking costumes. She also often used what little money she had to buy fresh flowers, which she would wear in her hair. Friends remembered that she would sometimes sleep in the flower market, where the sellers would gift her leftover bouquets, many believing that she was some kind of a saint or prophet.

Marsha's reputation as a legendary presence on the streets of the Village and beyond was already well established when, in June 1969, she became one of the main participants in the Stonewall riots. Although exact details of her involvement vary from account to account, there is no doubt that she was one of the most prominent activists in the early gay liberation movement. She was also one of the first drag queens to frequent Stonewall in the months predating the riots—the bar had previously exclusively catered to cis gay men. Following Stonewall, Marsha became even more heavily involved in activism, joining the Gay Liberation Front and marching at the head of the first-ever gay pride rally on the first anniversary of Stonewall. Alongside her friend and fellow trans activist legend Sylvia Rivera, Marsha established STAR (Street Transvestite Action Revolutionaries), the first organization designed to protect trans youth of color. Johnson and Rivera managed to secure a building on East Second Street, known as the STAR House, which became a safe haven for homeless trans and queer youth who had often been rejected by their families and were especially vulnerable to violence.

Despite her growing profile, Marsha continued to live the life of a street queen. Throughout the 1970s she stayed active in the movement while also working as an entertainer, and she continued to engage in sex work. During that time she posed for Andy Warhol, who immortalized Johnson's image as part of his iconic series of portraits of transgender street queens entitled "Ladies and Gentlemen."

While working on the streets, Marsha was often a victim of violence, both at the hands of her clients and by the police, and she was arrested numerous times. Although universally known as a warm and happy presence on the gay scene, she also suffered from periodic bouts of depression and would at times voluntarily seek help at mental health facilities, where she would sometimes spend weeks recuperating. During the 1980s and the AIDS pandemic, Johnson became known for her compassion in caring for friends infected with the virus as well as for visiting the sick in hospitals and staying at their bedside. She later tested HIV positive herself and openly talked about her diagnosis and the stigma and suffering experienced by the community.

Marsha died in 1992, her body found floating in the Hudson River just off the Christopher Street Pier. The death sent shock waves through the community, and although

"Darling, I want my gay rights now!"

the official ruling proclaimed suicide, few believed it to be the case. At the time, anti-LGBTQ+ violence was rampant, especially among trans women of color—something that sadly remains true to this day. While Marsha's life and heroism represent the individual courage shown by her and many other activists, her death has come to symbolize the wider, ongoing problems faced by the LGBTQ+ community. She is the face of the faceless, the voice of the voiceless, an icon who reminds us all of the sacrifices of the past, of the achievements of those who came before us, risking and often offering their own lives for a brighter future. But Marsha's legacy and death also serve as a reminder that our work is far from done: until every member of our community enjoys freedom and safety, there is no time to rest.

Totally outrageous and unpredictable, Divine revolutionized what it meant to be a drag queen, reshaping the concepts of camp and comedy. Initially inspired by the movie queens of his youth, including Elizabeth Taylor and Marilyn Monroe, Divine set out to create a world where he could exist as a woman every inch as fabulous as the glamorous stars of Hollywood cinema—but bigger. Much, much bigger. In fact, for none of the icons is the title "larger than life" more fitting than it is for Divine. With such cult classics as *Pink Flamingos*, *Female Trouble*, *Polyester*, and *Hairspray*, all directed by underground master John Waters, Divine truly earned his place among the most iconic figures of queer culture.

Growing up a chubby kid in Baltimore, the future Divine was bullied for his size and effeminate manner. As for millions of other queer teenagers of the time, coming out was not an option. Glenn's dream of becoming a movie star, in the vein of those he so admired—Elizabeth Taylor, Mae West, Marilyn Monroe, and Jayne Mansfield—seemed about as possible as flying to the moon. It is perhaps not a coincidence then that mankind's giant leap in 1969 would also coincide with the rise of Divine—undoubtedly a huge milestone in the history of queerness.

Meeting John Waters changed Glenn's fortunes. Waters, who lived in the same neighborhood, introduced Glenn to the radical, arty circles of Baltimore's youth counterculture, and the two soon began to experiment with producing homemade movies, in which Glenn first adopted a drag persona. The name Divine was Waters's idea; it toyed with established notions of female beauty and boldly distorted them. The pair's reputation steadily grew, mostly due to the irreverent and outrageously provocative humor they injected into their experimental movies. But it was Divine's charisma and campy glamour that drew the most attention. While drag culture already existed, it was traditionally designed to emulate feminine appearance to the point where it was difficult to distinguish whether the actor was indeed female or a male in drag. Divine had no interest in the pageantry of drag; he saw himself as a character actor, and the persona he invented was designed to entertain and shock rather than simply exist for aesthetic pleasure. His large size also contributed to the shock value; plus-sized drag queens were as rare as plus-sized fashion models, and Divine's unapologetic approach to his body smashed barriers for other drag artists who followed.

By 1972, Divine's name was well established on the underground scene, but it was with the release of Waters's *Pink Flamingos* that year that a cult icon was truly born. The movie became an unexpected hit on the midnight screening circuit, helping to popularize the practice of screening low-budget and underground movies in movie theaters around the country. *Pink Flamingos* became notorious as the movie in which Divine apparently consumes dog feces, a scene that would go on to haunt him for the rest of his life. Despite protest and outrage, the film received a good deal of positive critical attention and became an undisputed cult classic. Perhaps few people at the time could have predicted that a half-century later *Pink Flamingos* would be selected for preservation by the Library of Congress.

The success of the film brought Divine national attention, and he became perhaps the first celebrity drag queen. Following a starring role in the next Waters vehicle, *Female Trouble*, which also proved a success, Divine moved to New York, where he became a fixture on the scene, mingling with Andy Warhol and others. He was frequently photographed partying at Studio 54, always in full drag, exuding the very particular brand of Divine glamour. Although grateful for the success and recognition, Divine also longed to be regarded as more than just a drag persona; he wanted to be seen as a skilled actor. To that end, he starred in a number of off-Broadway productions, including the highly successful *Women Behind Bars*, in which he played a predatory female prison warden.

Divine's fame grew throughout the 1970s and early '80s, with multiple club tours and personal appearances and a number of pop records, including the camp classics "You Think You're a Man" and "Walk Like a Man." The demands of touring and performing his high-energy sets, as well as his increasing weight problems, took an enormous toll on his health. Those close to him, including Waters, expressed concern, but Divine's drive to carry on and perform was too strong to allow him to slow down.

In 1981, Divine's childhood dream of becoming a leading lady in the tradition of his favorite classic Hollywood stars came true when he appeared opposite another gay icon and former screen idol, Tab Hunter, in Waters's satire *Polyester*. The film was a spoof of the popular "women's pictures" of the forties and fifties as well as the melodramas of Douglas Sirk, and with the unlikely pairing of Divine and Hunter it became a camp fest for the ages. The film was a success, even receiving positive reviews from the mainstream press, and it led to another collaboration between Divine and Tab Hunter, the 1985 western

"I think the least of people's worries is a man in a dress."

comedy *Lust in the Dust*. Divine's last and biggest success came with the 1988 John Waters comedy *Hairspray*. It was the first time Divine would play a supporting role in a Waters movie, and his usual outrageous glamour was replaced with a highly unflattering look designed for the character of Edna Turnblad. Despite this, Divine received the best notices of his career and was nominated for an Independent Spirit Award. The film's success solidified his status as a star and a camp icon. Divine's lifelong dream of being accepted as a character actor finally came true when he was cast in a male role on the hit TV show *Married . . . with Children*; he died the night before his first shooting day.

The legacy of Divine lives on. His iconic status as a larger-than-life queen opened the doors for an entire new wave of drag artists, bringing comedy and irreverent humor to what had previously been seen largely as purely decorative art. Divine also achieved something that has never been done before or since: he became a full-fledged drag queen movie star. While privately he might have at times struggled with being trapped inside the brilliant persona he had created, the queer community will never cease to be grateful for the trail he blazed for all of us.

ANDY
WARHOL

An instantly recognizable figure in contemporary art, Andy Warhol almost single-handedly developed the idea of pop, highlighting the fickle nature of modern celebrity culture. As a queer icon, he helped to shape the iconography of other legendary names by including them in his visual world—from his representations of Marilyn, Elizabeth Taylor, and Liza to his Polaroid snapshots of street queens and trans people, Warhol's vision of the LGBTQ+ community and its icons has become an invaluable part of the queer narrative. His own personal style and the mystique surrounding his intimate life only add to the overall fascination that Warhol continues to arouse, more than three decades after his death.

Andy Warhol's unique vision of the world, seen through the prism of glamorous images and mass-produced symbols of modern consumerism, totally revolutionized the way art is viewed and created. But the queer sensibility profoundly embedded into his work also makes his legacy unique and enduring. Though never involved in the gay liberation movement, Warhol lived his life as an openly gay man, even in the years before Stonewall. He came to embody the very idea of queerness as the ultimate figure of a queer artist, an image many aspired to and many despised.

Brought up in a poor immigrant family in a working-class neighborhood in Pittsburgh, Warhol was a shy, sickly child deeply self-conscious about his looks. He grew up in a religious atmosphere, and the Catholic imagery that surrounded his childhood would continue to play an important role in shaping his artistic sensibilities, remaining one of his chief inspirations for the rest of his life. Warhol was also fascinated by celebrity, and commercial images would, for him, become the modern equivalent of religious imagery. Throughout the 1950s Warhol lived in New York, where he worked as a successful commercial illustrator, further developing his interest in the power of image in advertisement.

In wasn't until the 1960s that he started being widely noticed and recognized as one of the most interesting artists on the scene. In November 1962, just two months after her death, Warhol first introduced his now-iconic images of Marilyn Monroe at an exhibition of his work held at the Stable Gallery in Manhattan, alongside works depicting Campbell's soup cans, Coke bottles, and dollar bills—all of which were to become his signature motifs. The exhibition helped to propel Warhol to fame, and for the rest of the decade he would continue to create iconic images of classic Americana as well as scenes of violence, all of which brought him a great deal of attention as his works became emblematic symbols of the 1960s and the growing pop-art movement.

During that time, Warhol also founded a studio and artists' collective called the Factory. As well as attracting young artists from around the country, it would also come to represent a safe space for queer people, including trans women. During this era, which many consider to be his golden age, Warhol experimented with filmmaking, producing numerous under-ground movies starring some of his favo-rite muses, including transgender icons like Candy Darling and Holly Woodlawn. He also managed and produced the iconic band the Velvet Underground, which became the Factory's official house band.

Warhol's intimate relationship with the gay underground constitutes one of the main pillars of his art. From the very early days of his career, his work was noted for its homoerotic nature and queer imagery. While Warhol drew heavily from gay culture, he simultaneously contributed to it. His images of queer icons, such as Marilyn, Judy, Liz, and Liza were both a celebration and a confirmation of their status. Many of his experimental movies of the 1960s, including *Blow Job* (1964), which Warhol maintained was performed by "five beautiful boys," were screened at gay porn theaters.

In later years, Warhol would return to the underground LGBTQ+ scene of New York for inspiration. In 1975, he created the series *Ladies and Gentlemen*, which depicted Black and Hispanic drag queens from the Greenwich Village scene. Warhol would take Polaroid photos of the queens in his studio, then transform them into colorful prints. It was significant that Warhol, by this point one of the most established artists in the world, chose to celebrate some of the most marginalized members of the queer community, though in the years since some have argued that he exploited underprivileged performers by using their images to increase his own popularity and vast fortune. Yet there is no denying that *Ladies and Gentlemen* was a bold artistic statement at a time when queer visibility in the mainstream was still incredibly low. His portraits subvert traditional gender roles, questioning the notions of beauty and celebrating racial diversity. One of the models for the series was Marsha P. Johnson, though at the time all the portraits were presented as anonymous figures. It is not clear whether Warhol was fully aware of the extent of Johnson's status as an activist and an icon in her own right within the queer community.

"Art is what you can get away with."

In the 1980s Warhol's popularity experienced a renaissance, thanks to the emergence of the MTV generation and a new wave of young artists who idealized him. His work and his contribution to the increased visibility of the queer community were reevaluated, and Warhol began to collaborate with other artists, most notably Jean-Michel Basquiat. With his unexpected death in 1987, Warhol entered the sphere of pop culture mythology—a sphere he himself helped to create. His work continues to grow in popularity, with many of his pieces fetching record-breaking sums at auctions around the world. But through it all, Warhol himself remains an enigma. His attitudes to life and sex, as well as his personal relationships, continue to be the stuff of legend. And while we may never fully know and understand the man behind the art, what remains undisputed is Andy Warhol's legacy as a queer icon and a groundbreaking artist, whose fame will last far beyond the fifteen minutes he prophesied for future celebrities.

EARTHA KITT

With her distinctive, sultry purr, sexy stage persona, and outspoken activism, Eartha Kitt was idolized by the LGBTQ+ community throughout her long career. Often misunderstood and even persecuted for her open-mindedness and liberal attitudes, Kitt knew what it meant to be a social outcast. "I feel very close to the gay crowd because we know what it feels like to be rejected," she once said. Whether recording her instantly recognizable hits, performing on stage, or playing Catwoman, Eartha Kitt was never anything less than a bona fide icon.

Everything about Eartha Kitt screamed queer icon: her campy appearance; her distinctive way of delivering song lyrics; her unapologetic views on everything from politics and gay rights to romantic relationships; and her unhappy, traumatic childhood, which she overcame with her characteristic grit to become one of the most successful entertainers of her era.

From the rural South, Kitt was born to a Black-Cherokee mother and an unknown, most probably white father. From the get-go, she faced prejudice. Her stepfather rejected her for being too white, and she was sent to live with relations. She was subjected to abuse and maltreatment, dreaming of escape and a better life elsewhere. Her chance came when she was sent to live with her aunt in New York City, where she enrolled at a performing arts high school. Studying dance and voice, she quickly distinguished herself with a rare mix of talent and nonchalant sex appeal. One of those impressed by the young performer was Orson Welles, who cast her as Helen of Troy in his production of *Doctor Faustus*, later proclaiming her to be "the most exciting woman in the world."

At a time when entertainers of color faced an uphill struggle, Kitt managed to overcome many of the limitations placed upon her by the industry, and by the early 1950s she was one of the most famous singers in the country. From the earliest days, she had attracted queer audiences, exhibiting an unusual quality of naughtiness and defiance that stood in contrast with the good girls like Doris Day and Rosemary Clooney. With such legendary hits as "Santa Baby" and "I Want to Be Evil," Kitt projected a persona that gay men in particular responded to, establishing her as an early queer icon—a status she would maintain for the rest of her life.

As well as her successful recording career, Kitt worked in movies and television and became a legendary nightclub performer. In 1967 she starred as Catwoman in the third season of the original *Batman* TV series, securing a cult following among fans of the comic book character. Throughout the fifties and sixties she was an outspoken supporter of the civil rights movement, and she worked tirelessly with underprivileged youth. She was also one of the most vocal opponents of the Vietnam War, causing major controversy with her remarks during a 1968 White House luncheon. She reduced Lady Bird Johnson to tears with her remarks, which included the statement: "The children of America are not rebelling for no reason. They are not hippies for no reason at all. You have children of your own, Mrs. Johnson— we raise children and send them to war." The incident derailed her career, though she was considered an icon by the antiwar movement.

During the 1970s she continued to perform, mainly in Europe and Asia, before making a triumphant return to Broadway in 1978. Her status as a queer icon strengthened in the 1980s, when she became a staunch supporter of LGBTQ+ rights. "After my blacklisting, it was the gay community that welcomed me back with open arms," she stated. Kitt made numerous appearances in support of HIV/AIDS organizations, and she toured gay clubs with her act, which by now also included disco hits like "Where Is My Man" and "Cha-Cha Heels." Her increasingly camp aesthetic made her a favorite among a new generation of queer fans, but she also maintained her older fandom, which had stayed loyal since her first hits in the early fifties.

Though Kitt had never known the love and warmth of a family, she knew how important it was to find comfort and safety within a community of supportive and like-minded people, which is why she shared such an intimate understanding with the LGBTQ+ community. Always sensitive to prejudice and discrimination, she became one of the first celebrities to speak out in favor of marriage equality. "We were not allowed to go through certain doors because of our race, our color," she once said. "It was so stupid that we were not able to sit at the counter of a restaurant because it was only for Anglo-Saxons. It's stupid when this country says it was born on 'freedom for all,' but it's 'freedom for some.' I support gay marriage because we're asking for the same thing. If I have a partner and some-thing happens to me, I want that partner to enjoy the benefits of what we have reaped together. It's a civil right thing, isn't it?"

Kitt worked until the end of her life, earning rave reviews and a string of awards, including three Daytime Emmy Awards and two Tony nominations. She left this world a better place than she found it, and her rich legacy as an iconic star and fierce activist continues to inspire. Hers was a purr heard round the world.

"I stayed on my own path
and did not follow the herd.
I made a way for myself."

CHER

Cher is without a doubt one of the greatest queer icons of all time. Establishing her status as early as the 1960s, she has not only managed to maintain it throughout the decades but has grown her stature with groundbreaking achievements in the entertainment industry, her bold style, and her unwavering support for the LGBTQ+ community. Cher's evolution as an artist and as an icon has closely paralleled the time line of the gay rights movement, starting in the years before Stonewall and continuing through the decadent days of disco, the dark period of the AIDS crisis, and into the modern era of triumphant milestones. Through it all, Cher has proven that much like the community that so embraced her, she is a survivor, defying societal rules and limitations and emerging as the ultimate symbol of unconventional fabulousness.

It is almost impossible to talk about Cher without considering her status as a beloved queer icon. In many ways she is the ultimate one. Her countless career achievements—as an acclaimed actor, one of the best-selling recording artists of all time, a legendary concert performer, a pioneering style icon—are inextricably linked to her gay following. "Gay people don't feel like they fit in, and I never felt like I fit in," she once reflected.

For Cher the sense of not belonging, so often experienced not only by LGBTQ+ people but also by those they choose as their icons, started when she was a child growing up in suburban California. She dreamed of stardom yet felt discouraged by the established standards of beauty she was surrounded by. No one in the movies looked like her. This sense of otherness would one day prove to be the basis of her signature style: unconcerned by existing conventions, always on the forefront of change. At the age of sixteen, she dropped out of school and moved to Los Angeles, seeking to take charge of her own destiny. She wasn't quite sure what direction to take, but she knew she wanted to achieve fame. Her early records, produced by Phil Spector, whom she met through Sonny Bono, were often turned down by radio DJs, who believed they were love songs sung by a gay man. Undeterred by the early rejections, Cher would soon find success as one half of the pop duo she formed with Bono. The two also became romantically linked, eventually marrying in 1969. Their break-through hit, "I Got You Babe," became one of the defining anthems of the early sixties. Their popularity quickly waned, however, and by the end of the decade they were seen as too soft to appeal to the Woodstock generation. It wouldn't be the last time that Cher was written off by the industry, and she soon showcased her incredible power of self-resurgence, an ability she would demonstrate countless times through the coming decades.

Cher's first comeback occurred during the seventies with the *Sonny and Cher Comedy Hour*, which showed a new side of Cher's persona. It was also during that time that she collaborated with the gay designer Bob Mackie, who created her unforgettable and instantly iconic looks. Her relationship with Mackie would last for years, producing some great fashion moments and helping to establish her as a flamboyant queer icon. She also made a successful return to music, releasing a string of hit songs, including such queer anthems as "Gypsies, Tramps and Thieves," "Dark Lady," "Half-Breed," and "Take Me Home." During this time Cher became one of the emblematic icons of the disco era, with her instantly recognizable look emulated by drag artists and embraced by legions of queer fans.

By the 1980s, Cher's star persona had undergone another major transformation. She had changed her image from a disco goddess to a more edgy rock star, and she also set out to break into movies. Few believed that Cher's outrageous persona would translate well to cinema, and she remembered people laughing at the sight of her name in the trailer for her first movie, *Come Back to the 5 & Dime, Jimmy Dean, Jimmy Dean*. Soon no one laughed, as Cher proved herself to be a highly talented and versatile screen actor, with acclaimed performances in *Silkwood* (1983), which brought her an Academy Award nomination for Best Supporting Actress, and *Mask* (1985). Two years later she achieved the pinnacle of movie stardom, appearing in three hit movies in the same year: *The Witches of Eastwick*, *Suspect*, and *Moonstruck*, the last of which won her the Best Actress Oscar. She collected her award in a see-through black gown, designed once again by Mackie, and declared: "This doesn't mean that I am somebody, but I guess I'm on my way."

By the time she won her Oscar, Cher had achieved "living legend" status, and in the LGBTQ+ community in particular she was seen as an iconic goddess. She continued to strengthen her gay following with such unforgettable moments as her 1989 music video for "If I Could Turn Back Time" (which showed her performing aboard the battleship *Missouri*, wearing the skimpiest of outfits, surrounded by cheering marines), and her role in *Mermaids* (1990), which featured "The Shoop Shoop Song." Her position was further enhanced by her fourth major musical comeback with the global hit "Believe" in 1998, which became one

"All of us invent ourselves. Some of us just have more imagination than others."

of the best-selling singles of all time and introduced Cher to a whole new generation of fans. The success of "Believe" cemented the notion that Cher was the ultimate phoenix of the entertainment industry, and the song's popularity on the gay scene reaffirmed Cher's image as one of the greatest queer icons ever. She continued to break records with her concert tours and residencies, recordings, and appear-ances in such queer favorites as *Burlesque* (2010), opposite Christina Aguilera, and *Mamma Mia: Here We Go Again* (2018).

After more than six decades of stardom, Cher is still a force to be reckoned with, and her legacy is secure. As a mother of a trans man, Chaz Bono, she is also one of the most visible and outspoken advocates for the community.

One of the most striking and unconventional stars in show business, Grace Jones has enjoyed a devoted queer following since she made her recording debut in 1975 with "I Need a Man." Renowned as an androgynous, gender-defying diva with an unforgettable personal style and an unapologetically free spirit, Jones rose to prominence at the height of the Studio 54 days, becoming one of the emblematic figures of that time of delicious decadence. As a singer, actor, and model, she continued to shatter barriers beyond the disco era, inspiring entire trends both in music and fashion and securing a legacy as an important and endlessly fascinating LGBTQ+ icon.

Growing up in an ultrareligious environment, first in her native Jamaica and then in Syracuse, New York, Grace Jones had plenty to rebel against from an early age. Her desire to break free from stifling conventions eventually propelled her to international fame. As a teenager, she began experimenting with drugs and wearing makeup, and she frequented gay clubs with her brother, who himself struggled with his sexuality. It soon became clear that she couldn't stay at home with her conservative and disapproving parents, so at eighteen she moved to New York City. Even at such a young age, she possessed an air of confidence and sophistication and gave the impression that she had already lived many lives. Gifted with striking good looks, which blended statuesque femininity with distinct masculine elements, she was signed as a model by the Wilhelmina agency. Despite her potential, she initially found little success and in 1970 decided to move to Paris.

Jones was one of many beautiful and adventurous young people who had descended upon Paris in the late sixties and early seventies. The city was bursting with creative energy and manic excitement. Her looks and attitude quickly earned her a reputation as one of the most popular young models in the city, and she was soon friends with Jessica Lange, a future Oscar winner and a gay icon, as well as Jerry Hall. In Paris Jones's artistic sensibility was truly formed— the city gave her the confidence to reach higher than just modeling. She knew she wanted more. "We all had ambition to be more than models," she later wrote. "We all wanted to be fabulous in different ways." And fabulous she certainly was. It was difficult to overlook her stunning ebony beauty, and she soon became a muse for a number of photographers and fashion designers,

BORN: GRACE BEVERLY JONES, MAY 19, 1948, SPANISH TOWN, JAMAICA including Antonio Lopez and Karl Lagerfeld. It was also in Paris that Grace's queer icon status began forming—she would appear nightly at the city's trendiest gay spots, including the legendary Le Sept, and her androgynous, gender-defying looks made her a favorite in the community.

In 1975 Jones released her first club hit, "I Need a Man," which became a gay anthem and made her an instant star on the gay scene. In 1977 her first album, *Portfolio*, came out and was a success, particularly among the disco-loving queer community. She followed it with two more disco albums, *Fame* and *Muse*, and became an iconic figure of the era. A regular at Studio 54, her image became inseparably linked with the decadence of the late seventies. Grace's style of performance and striking, unconventional looks reinforced her iconic status for the gay movement, a standing that strengthened in the 1980s as she shifted her musical direction toward a more edgy New Wave sound. Though Grace's defiance of social norms and refusal to conform to traditional gender standards often shocked the mainstream, she was a trailblazer for other artists of the decade, including Annie Lennox and Boy George, who also played with established ideas of masculinity and femininity.

Grace's 1981 album *Nightclubbing* became a highly acclaimed success and is still considered one of the best records of the period. The song "Pull Up to the Bumper," with its suggestive lyrics and infectious beat, became a staple on the gay scene. She continued her success with hit albums like *Slave to the Rhythm* and *Island Life*, and she also branched out into acting, with roles in *Conan the Destroyer* (1984), opposite Arnold Schwarzenegger, and as a Bond villain in *A View to a Kill* (1984).

Grace's influence on popular culture has been enormous. Her unique style in fashion, music, and performance has inspired numerous artists, from Madonna to Lady Gaga. She helped to bring pop art into the mainstream, and as a friend and muse of Andy Warhol she is forever part of the movement's visual iconography. While her career slowed down during the 1990s, her status as a multifaceted icon has remained intact for the last four decades. In the LGBTQ+ community, she continues to be regarded as one of the most significant figures, with her legacy of promoting gender fluidity and breaking barriers and stereotypes, both racial and sexual.

More recently, Grace released the critically acclaimed album *Hurricane*, wrote a fabulous memoir, made a documentary film about her life (*Grace Jones: Bloodlight and Bami*), and hula-hooped for Queen Elizabeth's Diamond Jubilee while performing "Slave to the Rhythm." What could be more iconic than that?

"I feel feminine when I feel feminine. I feel masculine when I feel masculine. I am a role switcher."

ELTON

JOHN

From his flamboyant style to his legendary songs in a career that has spanned over six decades, Elton John has established himself as one of the most enduring and influential LGBTQ+ icons of all time. The Rocket Man, as he is known to his legions of fans, was one of the first prominent showbiz figures to come out, long before it was cool to do so, but as for so many in the community, his road to self-acceptance has been a long and difficult one. Along the way, he made history with countless artistic achievements, including number-one albums and record-breaking singles, movie soundtracks, and concert tours, and he is also one of the fiercest HIV/AIDS activists, with his foundation helping to raise millions for the cause every year.

There was nothing in Elton John's rigid, working-class upbringing in a small English town to suggest a future of fame and glory. Like so many of the icons in this book, Elton grew up longing for love and acceptance, struggling with feeling different from his peers. Music would prove to be his escape. A promising young pianist, at the age of fifteen he played piano and sang at a local pub. He decided to focus on developing a career in pop music, though he felt insecure because he didn't see many people who looked like him being represented in popular culture. From the beginning, he used flamboyant costumes to craft a more confident stage persona. His first major breakthrough came in 1967 when he met the lyricist Bernie Taupin. The two immediately hit it off and formed one of the most legendary songwriting duos in music history. While at first they created songs for other artists, they soon turned their focus to making Elton a star.

His first album, released in 1970 and simply titled *Elton John*, quickly established his reputation as a virtuoso of piano pop and included the timeless classic "Your Song." His meteoric rise to superstardom continued throughout the first half of the 1970s, with a record-breaking seven albums topping the charts within five years. The 1973 album *Goodbye Yellow Brick Road*, considered one of the best albums of that or any era, included the singles "Candle in the Wind" (dedicated to Marilyn Monroe) and "Bennie and the Jets." At the same time, Elton's glam rock image and exuberant manner of performance made him an iconic figure of the disco era and one of the most popular live artists in the world. In a 1976 interview with *Rolling Stone*, Elton came out as bisexual, making him one of the first public figures to do so. His openness about his own sexuality greatly increased the overall visibility of the LGBTQ+ community, and Elton, who had already enjoyed great popularity on the queer scene before, quickly rose to the status of an icon.

Throughout the 1980s he continued to release best-selling albums, with such iconic hits as "I'm Still Standing" and "Sacrifice." He took part in the legendary Live Aid concert at Wembley Stadium and also became one of the first musicians to speak out about HIV/AIDS and raise funds for AIDS research. In 1990 he teamed up with another iconic singer, George Michael, to perform "Don't Let the Sun Go Down on Me," and the two reunited in April of 1992 when they performed at the tribute concert for their friend Freddie Mercury, who had died of AIDS just months earlier. Also in 1992 Elton confirmed that he identified as a gay man, and he continued to be an outspoken supporter of his community. John's dedication to the AIDS cause includes the Elton John Foundation, which has raised more than $600 million for AIDS research. The annual Elton John Oscars party, which he has hosted on the night of the Academy Awards since 1993, is one of the most high-profile events in Hollywood's calendar and helps to raise millions for AIDS-related causes each year.

Elton John's iconic status only increased as the years rolled by. His soundtrack to the Disney classic *The Lion King* (1995) has become one of the most beloved of all time and led to John writing the phenomenally successful stage musical version of Simba's story. In 1997, in honor of Princess Diana, Elton and Taupin rewrote the lyrics to "Candle in the Wind" and performed the new version at Diana's funeral at Westminster Abbey, the only time John ever sang the Diana tribute version live. The studio recording went on to become the biggest-selling single of all time.

In the new millennium, Elton married his longtime partner, David Furnish, and the two became one of the greatest queer power couples in the world. Both continue to speak out on behalf of the community, and John is still seen as one of the fiercest advocates for queer youth and those living with HIV/AIDS. He is also still very much active as a performer and his influence on the world of music cannot be overestimated, with numerous artists citing him as a major influence. Yet it is his legacy as a trailblazing queer icon that may be his most incredible gift to the world.

"There is nothing wrong with going to bed with someone of your own sex."

DIANA
ROSS

Diva worship is an essential part of gay culture, and perhaps no other icon embodies the idea of a diva more than Diana Ross. Big hair, glamour, big personality, and decades of iconic hits—these are just some of the boxes this lady effortlessly ticks. But there is more to Ross the queer icon than meets the eye. Her music has been the soundtrack to gay life for half a century, with her 1979 song "I'm Coming Out" considered the ultimate anthem for the LGBTQ+ community. Add to it her film roles, legendary concert performances, and the embracing of her gay followers before it was fashionable, and you have yourself a true icon.

One spring day in 1996, Santa Monica Boulevard, the longest street in West Hollywood, was closed for several hours. The reason: Diana Ross was shooting her latest music video. Patrons of the gay clubs along the boulevard were encouraged to take part; everyone was welcome to join in. The song was a cover of Gloria Gaynor's "I Will Survive," one of the greatest gay anthems of all time, and the video was to feature numerous female impersonators dressed as Ross, as well as the most famous drag queen of them all, RuPaul. The queer extravaganza became an iconic video, but at the time no one in the country saw it. The music video never aired in the United States, an example of how homophobic attitudes persisted then as they persist today.

It wasn't the first time in her career that Ross raised eyebrows and risked being criticized for her association with the gay community. Nearly two decades before, in 1979, she had been told that the single "I'm Coming Out" would destroy her career, as it was perceived as a "gay song." Ross ignored the advice and released what is still considered the ultimate hymn of the LGBTQ+ community.

But the genesis of Diana Ross's queer icon status reaches even further back. As early as the 1960s, when she headed the successful Motown trio the Supremes, her glamorous persona attracted a gay following. Ross was a different kind of star, particularly for the queer community of color. At the height of that decade's racial tensions and struggle for civil rights, Ross stood for Black pride, the beauty of Black womanhood, and an icon for Black queers, who saw themselves marginalized both in their community and within the gay liberation movement.

Ross grew up in a Detroit housing project and dreamed of a career as a fashion designer. A talented singer, she joined an all-female vocal group, initially called the Primettes, and was discovered by her friend Smokey Robinson. The group was renamed the Supremes and became one of the most successful musical acts of the sixties, with twelve number-one hits. The star of the group, Ross left the Supremes in 1970 to pursue a solo career. From the start, the LGBTQ+ community constituted an important part of her fandom. Her first solo album, *Diana Ross*, proved that she was more than able to make it on her own, producing such hits as "Ain't No Mountain High Enough," a duet with Marvin Gaye that became her first number one post-Supremes.

Ross's fame grew throughout the seventies, as did her status as a queer icon, with further hit albums and an Academy Award–nominated performance in *Lady Sings the Blues* (1972), in which she portrayed Billie Holiday. Ross became one of the most prominent celebrities of the decade, appearing regularly at Studio 54 and epitomizing the glamour of the disco era. Her 1979 album *The Boss* became another gay favorite, but it was the release of her next single, "I'm Coming Out," in 1980 that propelled her to legendary status. The song's inspirational and uplifting lyrics made it an instant queer anthem, and it continues to be considered one of the most beloved LGBTQ+ affirming moments in popular music. Initially Ross didn't realize the impact the song would have on the gay community, thinking of it

instead as a way of announcing a new direction in her musical career, but she soon embraced its significance and has since performed it at a number of LGBTQ+ events.

By this point Ross was one of the great gay icons of all time and a favorite among drag artists. Her live performances were famous for their over-the-top glitz and glamour and were often seen as gay events in themselves. In 1983 she appeared at a free concert in New York's Central Park. The event, which occurred over two nights, has become legendary, particularly the first night, during which Ross performed to a huge crowd in the pouring rain. The image of the star, soaked to the bone and yet still glamorous, became part of her iconic history. "The sky darkened and the rain came, and it was the most incredible thing I had ever seen," Andy Warhol wrote in his diary. "It was like the greatest scene from a movie ever. And it was like a dream. A hallucination. Watching this spectacle."

Diana Ross has maintained her status for more than six decades and remains a powerful, glamorous presence. There is no doubt that she paved the way for other pop divas, but she has also created an image that has allowed queer people to feel more visible. "It's the most beautiful compliment," she said of the drag queens dressed up as her on the set of that infamous "I Will Survive" video in West Hollywood. The affirmation of her queer fans has secured her legacy as one of the quintessential LGBTQ+ icons.

"It takes a long time to get to be a diva. I mean, you gotta work at it."

FREDDIE MERCURY

Freddie Mercury was a bona fide diva, and with his flamboyant stage appearances, big personality, and that legendary voice, he remains one of music's greatest stars. While not officially out during his lifetime, Freddie came to symbolize the queer identity in mainstream culture, and from his camp aesthetic, which ranged from full-on drag to leather bear, to his artistic contributions, he was a trailblazer for the entire community. Immortalized in the catalog of numerous rock masterpieces created with his band, Queen (the name itself a humorous nod to queer identity), three decades after his tragic death from AIDS Freddie Mercury continues to shine as a true LGBTQ+ icon.

Freddie Mercury's musical legacy is one of the most significant contributions to popular culture ever made by an LGBTQ+ figure. His work and image constitute a vital part of our queer identity, even if Freddie himself never publicly aligned himself with the community. His sexual identity was of course the subject of rumors, and many friends have since claimed that Freddie was openly gay, but the fact remains that he chose not to make his sexuality public knowledge. Part of this was no doubt out of consideration for his Zoroastrian parents, who believed homosexuality to be akin to Satan worship. But it is also a testament to the wider cultural climate of homophobia of the time. The fact that Mercury, and millions of other less famous queer individuals, did not feel safe in disclosing their true identity is clear evidence of the discrimination the community faced.

It is perhaps tragically fitting that the life of the greatest queer star of his generation should be claimed by the dark plague of AIDS. His death in 1991 elevated Freddie's status to an emblematic queer icon and the famous face representing countless others dying of AIDS. His death, as well as his life and work, inducted him forever into LGBTQ+ iconography—something he perhaps couldn't have predicted.

Born in the British protectorate of Zanzibar and raised mostly in India, where he attended English-style boarding schools, young Freddie was fascinated by Western pop music and displayed extraordinary skill at playing any melody he heard on the piano. In 1964, Freddie and his family moved to England, where he studied art and design and attempted to break into the music industry, joining a succession of rock bands, all of which would prove short-lived. It wasn't until 1970 that Freddie, along with his friends Brian May and Roger Taylor, established Smile, a band that was later joined by John Deacon and, at Freddie's insistence, renamed Queen.

As the primary songwriter for Queen, Freddie wrote many of the band's iconic hits, including "Bohemian Rhapsody," "Killer Queen," "Somebody to Love," and "We Are the Champions." The band quickly became successful, and Freddie's flamboyant stage presence and camp aesthetics made him a star. Over the next decade his style evolved, slowly moving away from a glam rock persona and into a more individualistic look that incorporated many of the elements of gay underground culture. While many of Queen's straight, mainstream fans were unaware of Freddie's sexual identity, looking back today it is clear how much he was influenced by the queer aesthetic. As a result, Queen's sound also bears an undeniable stamp of queerness—many have pointed to "Bohemian Rhapsody" as the ultimate coming-out anthem.

But Freddie was more than a passive observer of queer culture. He was also an active participant, famous for his love of gay clubs, drag, and a very active sexual life. Although he maintained that the most meaningful relationship of his life was the one he shared with Mary Austin—a woman he lived with between 1970 and 1976 and remained close friends with afterward—

many who knew him well, including Austin herself, speculate that Freddie was a gay man. His involvement in the gay scene informed many of his visuals, including the classically queer music video for Queen's "I Want to Break Free," in which all members of the band appear in drag, a bold move at the time. The influences of queer culture are even more evident in Freddie's solo work, including his song and music video for "Living on My Own," in which he pays homage to another queer icon, Greta Garbo. The music video includes footage from Mercury's thirty-ninth birthday party in Munich and is in effect a huge, fabulous drag ball.

While his personal relationships with men were kept a secret from the public, they were well known among his friends and collaborators. The same was not true of his AIDS diagnosis. Freddie made sure that few knew about his health struggles, although he is said to have contracted the virus around 1987, with some speculating it might have appeared as early as 1982. While he continued his success with Queen, personally he faced the hardships shared by legions of gay men who suffered from the disease, though unlike many of them, Freddie had the means to afford the best medical care. What he was not able to rise above, however, was the stigma associated with HIV and those who carried it. This nightmare plagued him until the day he died. Just twenty-four hours

"I always knew I was a star. And now, the rest of the world seems to agree with me."

before his passing, Freddie finally put an end to months of media speculation, releasing a statement in which he admitted to being HIV positive. A day later, he was gone.

Freddie's deathbed admission was significant: it would help to fight the stigma and afford those who suffered from AIDS the dignity they had been denied throughout the 1980s. In the immediate aftermath of Freddie's death, the narrative in the public discourse on AIDS shifted, along with the outpouring of love for Freddie and his music. In the spring of 1992, just months after Freddie's passing, a historic event took place at Wembley Stadium, where countless world-famous artists came together to pay tribute to Freddie Mercury and to raise awareness about AIDS. Among those who performed were other queer icons: Elton John, George Michael, Liza Minnelli, and David Bowie. Elizabeth Taylor spoke before an audience of seventy-two thousand people gathered in the stadium and millions more watching on TV screens around the world, perfectly summing up what was in everyone's hearts:

"We are here to celebrate the life of Freddie Mercury," she opened. "An extraordinary rock star who rushed across our cultural landscape like a comet shooting across the sky. We are here also to tell the whole world that he, like others we have lost to AIDS, died before his time. The bright light of his talent still exhilarates us, even now that his life has been so cruelly extinguished. It needn't have happened. It shouldn't have happened. Please, let's not let it happen again."

BETTE
MIDLER

It doesn't get much more iconic than performing in a gay bathhouse, and that's precisely how the Divine Miss M got her start in the entertainment industry, singing at the legendary Continental Baths in New York City. What followed was a stellar career in music, theater, and film which has lasted for more than five decades and featured standout moments throughout. Her queer following has been steadfast all along, and Midler never forgot where she came from, still cherishing the nickname "Bathhouse Bette." Outrageous, funny, and more than a little camp, she is one of the most celebrated stars in the ranks of LGBTQ+ icons.

Picture this: a singer dressed up as a mermaid, riding around the stage in an electric wheelchair, singing "I Will Survive." This might give you a taste of the kind of performer Bette Midler was at the height of her camptastic career. But then again, it is difficult to pinpoint exactly what constitutes the height of Midler's career. Even by the fickle standards of Hollywood success, hers has followed a particularly irregular path.

Midler was brought up in Honolulu, where, as the only Jewish girl in a largely Asian community, she felt like an oddball. Being named after Bette Davis should have been some indication of things to come. Even at a young age Midler was single-minded and bubbly and had a flair for the dramatic. After a short stint in college she headed for New York, with a dream of a showbiz career. She studied drama and got some work on Broadway, but her true breakthrough came when she was hired as a singer at the Continental Bathhouse, a gay bathhouse club located in the basement of the Ansonia Hotel in Manhattan. Years later she joked that she hadn't quite realized what a gay bathhouse was and that she was just happy to get a paycheck.

Midler's irreverent humor and outrageous stage persona soon earned her a reputation as one of the most interesting young talents in New York, and she started appearing on television and touring with her act. Unlike most artists in this book, Midler became a gay icon before she became a mainstream star. It was the community's stamp of approval that led to her success outside of the gay scene. Following her highly successful time at the Continental, she recorded her debut album, *The Divine Miss M*, building on the persona she'd created at the Continental. The album became a smash hit, earning platinum status and scoring Midler a Grammy Award for Best New Artist. For the remainder of the 1970s, Midler's star continued to rise, with two more albums and appearances on TV and on stage. In 1979 she made her big-screen debut, starring in *The Rose*. The movie, loosely based on the life of rock star Janis Joplin, brought Bette an Academy Award for Best Actress.

Though she seemed to be on top of her game, after *The Rose* Midler struggled to maintain the momentum she had enjoyed for almost a decade. While the music she released in the first half of the 1980s failed to match the success of her previous work, her work as a comedic actor brought her more acclaim. Her larger-than-life, hilarious persona, which had initially made her a star with queer audiences, now conquered the mainstream with such successful movies as *Down and Out in Beverly Hills* (1986), *Ruthless People* (1986), *Outrageous Fortune* (1987), and *Big Business* (1988). The same year she also starred in the hit drama *Beaches*, which, along with its theme song ("Wind Beneath My Wings") has become a queer cult classic.

Midler's career continued on a bumpy ride throughout the 1990s, starting with *For the Boys*, a musical about a 1940s singer who travels entertaining the troops during the Second World War. The film, which Midler coproduced, was roasted by critics and bombed at the box office, and Bette considered it a personal failure. Despite that, she won a Golden Globe for her performance and was nominated for her second Academy Award for Best Actress.

Disappointed with the reaction to *For the Boys*, she turned down the lead in *Sister Act* but later made a comeback with two major camp classics and queer favorites: *Hocus Pocus* (1993) and *The First Wives Club* (1996). Both movies continue to be enormously popular with new generations of LGBTQ+ people.

In the years that followed, Midler continued to be an important presence in the industry, touring, recording, and making occasional movie appearances, including supporting roles in the remakes of *Stepford Wives* (2004) and *The Women* (2008), both of which were critically panned. Bette continued to live up to her gay icon status, producing the Broadway show *Priscilla, Queen of the Desert* in 2011 and later returning to the stage herself in the Broadway hit *I'll Eat You Last: A Chat with Sue Mengers*. In 2017 she appeared in the Broadway revival of *Hello, Dolly!*, which became one of the biggest triumphs in her career and won her a Tony.

Bette Midler has come a long way since her days performing in the gay bathhouse, but what remains so lovable about her is that she is still Bathhouse Bette at heart. While we've seen plenty of outrageous, loud-mouthed wannabe icons come and go in the meantime, no one has ever been outrageous and loud-mouthed with quite as much fabulousness and style as the Divine Miss M. And for that, she has secured her place among the greatest queer icons we have.

"I wouldn't say that I invented tacky, but I definitely brought it to its present high popularity."

GEORGE MICHAEL

Initially seen as little more than a clean-cut, handsome teen idol, George Michael elevated himself to occupy a place among the most enduring and most defiant queer icons. Renowned for his voice, innovative visual style, and taboo-shattering lyrics, he has changed the way LGBTQ+ individuals are perceived in popular culture and beyond. His very public arrest for cruising in 1998, which was also his forced coming out, had the potential to ruin his career, especially after he chose to use the incident to highlight the antigay sentiment that permeated society at the time. Today George Michael remains one of the most beloved icons for the community of which he was such a visible and outspoken, even if initially reluctant, member.

During the 1990s, few pop stars held the sort of power over the collective imagination that George Michael did. His slick, highly stylized music videos perfectly reflected the era of supermodels and MTV, while George himself personified the highly sexual, liberated, and fluid image that we came to associate with this period. In private he struggled with his own sexuality, depression, and substance abuse. After a forceful and very public outing, he became an outspoken critic of hypocritical attitudes toward sexuality and queerness, establishing himself as one of the most prominent LGBTQ+ icons.

Born to an immigrant Greek Cypriot father and an English mother, George grew up in a loving yet strict environment and often struggled to fit in. While still at school he met his future Wham! partner, Andrew Ridgeley. The two formed the pop duo in 1981, and it soon became one of the most successful acts of the decade, with numerous hit songs, including "Freedom," "Wake Me Up Before You Go Go," "Last Christmas," and "Club Tropicana." Wham! catapulted George to the status of teen idol and sex symbol, and he was often seen as the bigger star of the duo. Michael and Ridgeley eventually parted ways in 1986, and George embarked on a solo career that would bring him even greater worldwide success.

From the beginning of his career as a solo artist, George employed a persona that incorporated many elements of the gay aesthetic, and although not officially out, his image evoked sexual ambiguity and appealed to the queer community. While the press endlessly speculated about his personal life, Michael chose not to disclose his queerness. At the same time, he was a fierce HIV/AIDS activist, and many point to the night of his performing "Somebody to Love" at the Freddie Mercury Tribute Concert in 1992 as the moment George Michael the gay icon was born. His impassioned, powerful performance captivated the 80,000-strong crowd at Wembley Stadium, and it electrified TV viewers around the world.

His triumphant appearance at Wembley was followed by a string of successful songs and a number of iconic music videos that set the standard for future pop stars. The clips for his songs "Freedom! 90," "Too Funky," and "Fastlove" were all groundbreaking. The first two featured some of the most famous models of the time, while "Fastlove," along with its provocative lyrics about sexual gratification without commitment, cemented Michael's status as one of the most provocative artists in the music industry. His 1996 album, *Older*, proved to be a huge commercial and critical success, especially in Europe. As a songwriter, producer, and musical arranger on the majority of his songs, George was always in full control of his own image, and at times the gay press, particularly in the United Kingdom, treated him with hostility. While he had faced pressures to come out for many years, it is easy to see

why for so long he chose not to. The intense homophobic attitudes of the eighties and nineties, made all the more pervasive by the AIDS crisis, were not conducive to a public coming out. Michael later explained that he was trying to protect his family, in particular his mother, from public scrutiny.

In 1998, after George was busted for cruising in a public toilet outside the Beverly Hills Hotel, his arrest led to an immediate and most public outing. Instead of letting the press shame him, Michael turned the narrative on its head. Almost overnight, he became not only one of the most famous members of the LGBTQ+ community but also one of its most passionate advocates. He addressed the incident with honesty and humor, appearing on a number of talk shows and later releasing the song "Outside." The single, along with its controversial music video, made headlines, but it was George who dictated how the story was represented. By refusing to deny or apologize, Michael opened the door for the idea that a global pop star and sex symbol could be queer, and that gay sex was not dirty.

While sales of his records increased after the arrest, the press scrutiny, along with the loss of his mother, as well as his partner to AIDS, took its toll on George, and he spent the next few years largely out of the spotlight. But there were still

"I have never and will never apologize for my sex life. Gay sex is natural, gay sex is good!"

great musical moments to come. In 2004 he released the critically lauded album *Patience*, and he continued to tour. His death at the age of fifty-three came as a shock to the world. While he had suffered from ill health for some time, no one saw the tragic end coming.

In death, as in life, George Michael remains an icon, and he will no doubt be remembered as one of the greatest pop stars of his generation. He is also an LGBTQ+ legend, symbolizing the perilous yet ultimately triumphant journey of self-acceptance all of us in the community still face.

PRINCESS DIANA

She was the People's Princess, the Queen of People's Hearts, a beloved icon who died tragically but who left an unparalleled legacy of love and kindness. Diana was a rebel who fought against the constraints of the powerful institution she had married into, and in the process she managed to rock many other boats. She has always enjoyed a special place among queer people—she understood many of our struggles, and she embraced the community at a time when few others in her position did. Like Judy and Marilyn, Diana came to represent both tender vulnerability and immense strength, navigating her way through hostile societal forces and eventually emerging victorious as an inspirational figure for the ages.

As the epitome of a person oppressed by society and familial structures, Princess Diana is a universally relatable figure across the LGBTQ+ community. But there is much more to her than being a victim; Diana was also strong, glamorous, funny, and intelligent, and her star quality shone brighter than any royal title bestowed upon her. As the heroine of the greatest real-life soap opera of the past century, Diana lived through the sort of public heartbreak that made queer people all around the world see something of their own struggles in hers. With her sudden, tragic death, she was instantly elevated to an immortal icon, a status reserved for very few.

Diana was born into privilege, or at least into material wealth. The daughter of Edward Spencer and his socialite wife, Frances Roche, Diana grew up on an enormous and historic estate, went to private schools, and by the age of nineteen owned her own flat in a posh London neighborhood. Emotionally, though, she was starved for love and affection. Her parents divorced when she was a little girl, and she was mostly raised by a succession of nannies and governesses and longed for the warm embrace of a real family. Although strikingly beautiful, she was shy and retiring, preferring walks in nature to grand society balls. Meeting Prince Charles, the heir to the British throne and the most eligible bachelor in the world, changed her life forever. Overnight, she became a global celebrity and the most desired subject of the paparazzi, who haunted her every step.

We all know what happens in this story: a beautiful, shy girl marries the prince and they live unhappily thereafter. Almost from the beginning of her public life, Diana was embraced by the queer community. In the bleak, oppressive years of Margaret Thatcher, she offered a ray of light, or perhaps a glimpse of a rainbow. She dressed flamboy-antly and was clumsy and spontaneous, always seemingly more at ease with ordinary people she met during her engagements than with royal circles. Her charisma and kindness were palpable. It was impossible not to love her.

And she returned the love, especially to those who needed it most. At the height of the AIDS crisis, Diana was the first royal to visit a hospital ward dedicated solely to those suffering from the disease. She also went further. The stigma attached to those with AIDS was extremely powerful, and many people still believed that they could get infected by touching or even being in the same room as an HIV patient. When Princess Diana walked into that hospital ward and took off her gloves to hold the hands of the sick, she sent a clear and enormously potent message to the world.

"AIDS doesn't make people dangerous to know, so you can shake their hand and give them a hug," she said in 1991. "Heaven knows they need it." By shaking the hands of the dying, mostly queer, patients, Diana created a powerful, lasting bond between herself and the LGBTQ+ community. It was a generous, heartfelt, and uncalculated act of kindness and empathy from a woman who herself needed those gifts. While she wasn't able to single-handedly remove the stigma of AIDS and the homophobic attitudes attached to it, she made an important advance in the right direction.

Throughout her life, Diana had many queer friends, and in private she found solace in those relationships, just as her public persona has been embraced by the gay community. There is the delicious, very possibly true legend of Freddie Mercury smuggling Diana dressed in drag into London's Royal Vaux-hall Tavern, one of the most iconic gay venues in the city. And then there were her close friendships with Gianni Versace, George Michael, and Elton John. Diana was a cool, progressive royal who not only tolerated queerness but embraced it, and who in many ways embodied it. While being a straight cis woman, Diana's life as a royal rebel and advocate of acceptance and love positioned her as a kind of honorary queer advocate—a role she carried off gracefully until the end of her life, proving that even without an official royal title, she was the true queen.

After her tragic death in the last days of the summer of 1997, the public outpouring of grief was unprecedented. People from all walks of life and all sexual orientations and gender identities felt the loss, but the LGBTQ+ community was especially touched by Diana's passing. When Elton John sang "Candle in the Wind" at her funeral, with lyrics rewritten to fit Diana's story, he forever linked her to the queer struggle. Today, more than twenty-five years later, Diana's iconic status continues to gain in strength as her life and legacy are reexamined, often through the lens of queerness.

"I don't go by the rule book . . .
I lead from the heart,
not the head."

The Queen of Pop has been one of the greatest queer icons for four decades. In a 1991 interview for *Good Morning America*, Madonna, at the time the biggest pop star in the world, declared, "What I think to be a big problem in the United States is homophobia." Statements like this were not something America was ready to swallow at breakfast, but Madonna never apologized for her opinions. Her voice was more than a breath of fresh air—it was a wind of change for an entire generation. For many queer people growing up in the 1990s, Madonna's documentary *Truth or Dare* was the first opportunity to see gay people represented on-screen.

Madonna was perhaps the first mainstream star to embrace and engage with her queer followers. As a young and impressionable student in Michigan, she was introduced to the gay clubs of Detroit by her mentor and dance teacher, Christopher Flynn. It was to be the beginning of a lifelong love affair with the LGBTQ+ community.

From the earliest days of her pop career, Madonna challenged convention and shocked with her frank and unapologetic approach to themes dealing with sex, gender politics, and queerness. Her music became the soundtrack of the marginalized, and her style and energy injected a much-needed dose of flamboyant color to the dark years of the AIDS crisis. Her early hits—including "Holiday," "Like a Virgin," and "La Isla Bonita"—established her as a nightclub favorite, but it was with her 1989 album

Like a Prayer and the empowerment song "Express Yourself" that Madonna truly entered the sphere of LGBTQ+ iconography. Her lyrics carried strength and encouragement, and her groundbreaking music videos showed her as powerful, highly sexual, and always in control. She was the kind of icon the queer community desperately needed in the wake of decade-long stigmatization by mainstream media and a large portion of the political establishment.

The relationship between Madonna and her LGBTQ+ followers has always been mutually beneficial. She has offered support and spoken on behalf of the community, receiving a devoted and loyal fan base and, more importantly, an endless source of inspiration in return. For the soundtrack of her 1990 film *Dick Tracy*, Madonna recorded a song inspired by the underground queer culture of New York, paying homage to a dance style that had been on the scene for a number of years. "Vogue," named after the dance, became a worldwide hit and has been credited with introducing the moves and attitude of "striking a pose" to the mainstream.

In the same year, Madonna embarked on her highly controversial Blond Ambition tour, traveling the world with a troupe of mainly gay dancers. The show was provocative and sexually explicit, but as ever, Madonna refused to compromise her vision. She openly spoke to her audiences about AIDS, homophobia, and the practice of safe sex, further enhancing her status as a leading ambassador for the LGBTQ+ community. A documentary film shot during those months introduced the world to the realities of gay life. The dancers featured in *Truth or Dare* achieved their own fame, becoming some of the first openly gay men represented in a widely shown documentary.

Through her nurturing, deeply personal approach to the young dancers, Madonna established herself as a symbolic mother figure, a protector for the queer community. While displaying her powerful Queen of Pop persona, she also showcased her vulnerable side: losing her mother at an early age and the difficult relationship with her father, as well as her unwillingness to conform to the norms of the heteronormative, conservative society. Her ability

to relate to the struggles of the gay community is deep and authentic and perhaps never more apparent than in the tender, most private moments she often shared with her dancers late at night after the show had ended.

Since then, Madonna has never backed down on her strong views or shied away from speaking out on behalf of the LGBTQ+ community. She has spent decades as a vocal advocate for the sufferers of AIDS, first getting involved the 1980s. Losing many friends to the disease, including Christopher Flynn, Madonna's dedication to the cause has been truly inspirational—as has been her brave stance against homophobia and transphobia, which she never fails to demonstrate. Whether performing her openly queer-friendly shows in Putin's Russia or delivering powerful speeches at award shows, Madonna is a fierce ambassador for the community.

Ever the mistress of reinvention, Madonna continues to make music embraced by queer listeners around the world. Her albums *Ray of Light*, *Music*, *Confessions on a Dance Floor*, *Rebel Heart*, and *Madame X* are considered as vital to gay culture as the lady herself, carrying lyrics filled with messages of hope and strength, while her videos and concert tours still constitute the blueprint for queer iconography.

When Madonna turned sixty in August 2018, the LGBTQ+ community around the

"Fighting for all marginalized people is a duty and an honor I could not turn my back on, nor will I ever."

world came together to pay tribute to the star who has been there for them throughout her career. In gay clubs and bars around the globe, weeklong celebrations took place, with her iconic music blasting out. While the younger generation might look to new stars for inspiration, Madonna will always remain the original rebel heart: a fearless, unstoppable force who shattered barriers and shone a light on the people and stories few cared to notice before.

WHITNEY HOUSTON

It's easy to see why the queer community embraced Whitney Houston: she was beautiful, glamorous, and gifted with a kind of voice that comes along only once in a generation. She could belt out heart-wrenching ballads and dance-floor fillers with equal ease, and she had that diva personality we love to worship. For nearly two decades, she reigned as the undisputed queen of the charts, breaking records and creating a new standard for those who followed in her footsteps. But there is also a darker, more painful side to her story, one shaped by tragedy and suppression, and it is perhaps that which has elevated Houston to the ranks of a timeless LGBTQ+ icon.

Whitney Houston's gay icon status long predates the explosive revelations of a 2018 documentary that suggested she was bisexual and had had a long-term relationship with her close friend Robyn Crawford. The fact that she was probably a member of the community only adds to her legacy as a queer favorite, a position she has held since the early days of her career.

It all started with the voice. It had the power to move anyone's heart, and yet beneath the confident belting was also hidden a note of sadness, a longing. Whitney sang of unfulfilled love, loss, loneliness. In all of her hits, she examines the hurdles of being on the outside of happiness, somehow a perpetual misfit. Even in her upbeat, club-friendly bangers like "I Wanna Dance with Somebody" and "How Will I Know," she is love's outcast. In her most powerful ballads, including of course "I Will Always Love You" and "I Have Nothing," she is vulnerable, familiar with pain and solitude. To be so gloriously beautiful and glamorous and yet so unhappy is perhaps the ideal recipe for becoming an enduring queer icon.

Whitney was destined to be a star. She came from a singing family: her mother, Cissy Houston, was a famed gospel singer, and the singers Dionne Warwick and Dee Dee Warwick were her first cousins. She grew up singing gospel in her local church, where it quickly became apparent that she had an extraordinary voice. She became a teen model and then a young pop star with her 1985 debut album, *Whitney Houston*, topping the charts and becoming an instant classic. The album was a major breakthrough and produced such hits as "Saving All My Love for You" and "Greatest Love of All."

Her second album, entitled simply *Whitney*, was an even bigger success and established Houston as a gay favorite, particularly after the release of the club smash "I Wanna Dance with Somebody (Who Loves Me)." The song struck a chord with the queer community, in part because of the ambiguous lyrics, and it continues to be seen as an important LGBTQ+ anthem. Other hit singles followed, including "Didn't We Almost Have It All," "So Emotional," and "Where Do Broken Hearts Go," all number-one hits.

Whitney's success continued throughout the remainder of the eighties, including her hit album *I'm Your Baby Tonight*, and she entered the new decade riding high. Though it was later revealed that throughout this period she was probably involved in a gay relationship with Crawford, Whitney never disclosed her sexuality, and in 1992 she married the R&B star Bobby Brown. Their turbulent relationship would play out very publicly, involving violent fights and drug use, ending Whitney's reputation as America's sweetheart. Personal heartache didn't stand in the way of her reaching new heights, however, as she transitioned to acting with the 1992 classic *The Bodyguard*. The film's soundtrack, which included Whitney's immortal rendition of Dolly Parton's "I Will Always Love You," became the best-selling soundtrack album of all time, and the song Whitney's ultimate hit.

Although troubles in her personal life continued to make headlines, Whitney powered on, creating some truly memorable musical moments in the process. Who can forget such queer favorites as "It's Not Right, but It's OK" from her album *My Love Is Your Love*, the ultimate diva collaboration with Mariah Carey, which also resulted in the hit "When You Believe." In 1999, she made a surprise appearance at the New York Lesbian and Gay Pride Dance, causing a sensation among crowds of her queer fans. Soon, however, her struggles and addiction to drugs became overwhelming, and she entered a period of professional decline and personal despair. She still made music, including releasing *Just Whitney* as well as a greatest-hits album, but the attention of the media focused on her private battles rather than on her artistic achievements.

For a while, it seemed that Whitney would fight her way back from the darkness. She divorced Brown, and her 2009 album *I Look to You* became a number-one hit. Her voice certainly bore the strain of the hardships she had gone through, and while she might not have hit the high notes she was so famous for, there was a new depth and wisdom to her delivery. Here was a woman who went through hell but came out the other side and was ready to face the future. Her strength was inspiring, and her new material was particularly embraced by the queer community. With Whitney's sudden passing on the eve of the Grammys in 2012, a legend was born. She was hailed as the voice of the century, a true star, and a groundbreaking trailblazer for Black artists and women in the music industry.

"When I decided to become a singer, my mother warned me I'd be alone a lot. Basically, we all are. Loneliness comes with life."

"If you can't love yourself, how the hell you gonna love somebody else?" With those words, queer icon RuPaul ends each episode of the groundbreaking, Emmy-winning TV show *RuPaul's Drag Race*. This simple mantra seems to encompass his entire life philosophy and his affirmative attitude, which helped to see the boy from San Diego through some dark days and establish him as the most successful drag performer in history.

It's impossible to overestimate the significance of RuPaul in bringing queerness and drag into the mainstream. Hailing from the underground club culture of the 1980s, where he mingled with exuberant, gender-bending performers, RuPaul emerged in the early 1990s as a major cultural phenomenon. Singing, dancing, and strutting his way to fame, he never apologized for who he was.

RuPaul grew up in a conservative community in San Diego, where he struggled to find acceptance and a sense of belonging. Seeking inspiration from iconic divas like Diana Ross, he moved to Atlanta, Georgia, at the age of fifteen to study art and performance. After dabbling in different artistic circles, he realized that drag was his destiny. Unlike Divine, who found success through the exploitation of the grotesque elements of drag, RuPaul embodied the dream of legions of queer and transgender people who hoped to be seen and taken seriously for exactly who they were. His concept of a "glamazon," a beautiful, highly glamorous drag queen, became a figure to be admired rather than ridiculed.

It is difficult now to appreciate the barriers faced by young drag performers before RuPaul's influence. The 1990 documentary *Paris Is Burning* featured young drag performers from Harlem dreaming of mainstream success, a dream that at the time seemed impossible to achieve. The film highlighted the painful reality of how limited the chances of succeeding were for anyone who wasn't straight and white. RuPaul proved it was possible to live that dream. After years of political oppression, the horrifying specter of AIDS, drug wars, homophobia, and racism, RuPaul became a beacon of hope and a tantalizing symbol of new possibilities when he released his first album, *Supermodel of the World*, in 1993. The song "Supermodel (You Better Work)," from that album, was shown regularly on MTV, signaling a sea change in the representation of queer people of color in the mainstream media.

While the majority of his devoted following remained rooted in the LGBTQ+ community, RuPaul broke through other barriers for drag performers. As well as having several successful dance albums, he became the first drag artist to model for a major cosmetics company (MAC) and landed his own talk show (*The RuPaul Show* on VH1, 1996–1998). With his catchy dance tunes and larger-than-life persona, he was already a well-established queer icon when *RuPaul's Drag Race* debuted on VH1 in 2009.

Initially seen as a low-budget spoof of other major network competition shows, such as *America's Next Top Model, Drag Race* became a runaway hit and a pop-culture phenomenon. For many viewers, the show provided the first-ever glimpse into the art of drag, which was still seen as a largely underground form of performance. Inspired by the drag balls of the 1980s, which RuPaul witnessed firsthand, the show was rooted in queer tradition, exploring the culture, language, and history of the community.

Perhaps most importantly, the show brought the voices and stories of queer people to the forefront. With many contestants struggling with homophobia, racism, transphobia, and the lack of acceptance from their families or religious communities, *Drag Race* became one of the most important platforms for LGBTQ+ representation in America. Over its decade-long run (and counting), *RuPaul's Drag Race* has changed the face of drag. Many of the show's participants followed in Mama Ru's footsteps, achieving a level of global success unimaginable for previous generations of drag artists.

Much more than a drag queen, RuPaul is a tireless advocate for the LGBTQ+ community and a champion of creative talent from diverse backgrounds. His own inspirational story and motivational attitude continue to serve as proof that the key to success is finding one's most authentic self and reaching for one's dreams, no matter how unattainable they might appear.

"We are all born naked,
and the rest is drag."

LADY GAGA

Lady Gaga's rise to stardom signaled a new era in queer culture, as she redefined what it meant to be an LGBTQ+ icon. Unlike those who came before her, for Gaga being a gay icon isn't merely something that accompanies her other traits as an artist; openly bisexual, she offers her allegiance to the queer community as the very essence of her star persona. From the beginning of her career, Mother Monster has been both a champion of and an inspiration for a whole generation of queers, through her art and her activism, and she has secured herself a lasting spot among the most significant entertainment figures in LGBTQ+ history.

In many ways, Lady Gaga is the cultural offspring of the great queer icons who came before her—Judy to Madonna, Barbra and Liza to Elton John, Andy Warhol, and Grace Jones. She has combined their legacies and made them into her own unique blend of fabulousness, which captivated the LGBTQ+ community from the very moment she stepped into the limelight. But there is more to Gaga's phenomenon than mere imitation or the rehashing of old ideas: she is in possession of true talent, a powerful voice, and, perhaps most important, the ability to connect and empathize with her fans. Initially, the main feature of her celebrity seemed to be her ability to shock with her outlandish costumes. However, it soon became apparent that she was much more than a shock queen. She was here to stay, and the most significant feature of her creative work would be the empowerment of those without a voice—most predominantly, those in the queer community.

Born and raised in Manhattan, Gaga was fascinated by music and performing from an early age and started learn the piano at age five. Her artistic sensibility was shaped by influences from pop artists like Madonna and Cher but also rock bands and glam-rock artists like David Bowie and Queen. Her place within the queer community reaches back to her earliest days of performing in underground clubs and experimental burlesque acts. She has credited LGBTQ+ audiences with helping to establish her career, and the close relationship between Gaga and her queer fans has strengthened through the years.

Her first album, *The Fame* (2008), became a global success, instantly elevating Gaga to stardom. The catchy dance numbers like "Just Dance," "Poker Face," and "Love Game," along with the powerful visuals of her videos and the unusual, campy style of her often outlandish costumes helped establish her as a favorite on the gay club scene. But it was more than just a passing attraction; from the onset, it was clear that the cult of Gaga in the queer community was to be a huge part of her success. And Gaga was vocal in her support of her own community. She embraced her fans in a very personal way, quite unlike pop stars before her.

Her status as a major icon for the queer community was cemented by the release of her song "Born This Way," which was designed as an anthem of self-love and affirmation for the LGBTQ+ community, as well as anyone who has ever felt excluded. While some viewed Gaga's patronage as exploitative, seeing it as a way of cashing in on her status and commercializing queer culture, for the majority of the community the song came to symbolize a new era of empowerment and visibility. The album of the same name followed, and it became another huge success, earning three Grammy nominations and becoming a best seller worldwide. Gaga subsequently established the Born This Way Foundation, which focuses on youth empowerment, and she has been an active spokesperson in campaigns against bullying, which victimizes so many LGBTQ+ teenagers. She has also taken part in numerous marches and queer-led campaigns and is an ambassador for the community that has embraced her as she has embraced it.

Like Cher, Barbra, and Liza before her, Gaga's presence hasn't been confined to music. She earned rapturous reviews, along with an Oscar nomination for Best Actress, for her performance in *A Star Is Born* (2018), another milestone in the creation of her legendary status. By choosing this particular role as her big-screen debut, Gaga put herself in the same category as Judy Garland and Barbra Streisand, who both starred in earlier versions of the story. Making *A Star Is Born* for our time, Gaga knew that she was also placing herself in the role of the iconic, all-around entertainer and gay icon of her generation. It is this shrewdness that has worked in her favor from the start. Gaga has that natural ability to choose exactly what her public wants at any given time, and what is exactly right for her. A dance diva, a powerhouse voice, a taboo breaker, a fashion icon, and now an acclaimed actress—Lady Gaga ticks all the boxes. But perhaps more significantly, she has never lost touch with her audience, and it is for that very personal connection she shares with her Little Monsters that she is so beloved. She is not some unattainable goddess of pop, an icon cold in her perfection. She is human, flaws and all, and that is precisely what makes her the queer icon of our time.

"Don't you ever let a soul in the world tell you that you can't be exactly who you are."

BRITNEY
SPEARS

When Britney Spears made her debut with the instantly catchy "Baby One More Time" back in 1998, few could have predicted that twenty-five years later she would be one of the most iconic entertainers in the history of pop culture. Among the many elements that make Britney such a beloved figure in the LGBTQ+ community is her music—pure pop gold and yet uniquely hers, with deeply personal undertones and her unmistakable voice. Then there are her well-documented personal struggles, which, in the tradition of Judy, Marilyn, and other queer icons who came before her, have made Britney relatable to a community that has known abuse and familial rejection better than anyone else.

The relationship between Britney Spears and her legions of devoted queer fans is a unique and deeply personal one. While Spears is a quintessential pop star, with all-American good looks and a baby voice, she is much more than meets the eye. As a cultural figure, her significance over the past two decades has been immense. She has become the symbol of all that is perilous and destructive about modern celebrity: the exploitation, the sexism, the infantilization and objectification —the list goes on. But through all her struggles, she has also come to represent that most powerful of commodities: hope. In defying the oppressive forces around her and emerging as a free, independent woman, Britney is a heroine for all those whose voices and whole lives have been stifled. It is perhaps because of this that an entire movement has been created to liberate her. The "Free Britney" movement, established by her largely queer fan base, was a way for her audience to show just how deeply they care about their idol. By helping to free Britney from the abusive system under which she has lived for a large part of her adult life, her fans have also offered a kind of liberating hope for themselves.

Born in Mississippi and raised in Louisiana, Britney grew up singing in church choirs, attending voice and dance lessons, and winning local talent contests. Her childhood was virtually over by the age of eight, as her mother moved Britney to New York, where she started taking her to auditions for TV shows and Broadway musicals. In 1992 she joined the Mickey Mouse Club, where she would star for the next two years alongside future stars Christina Aguilera, Justin Timberlake, and Ryan Gosling. After the show got canceled, Britney attended high school back in Mississippi, but her stint as a typical teenager was to be short-lived. In 1997 she was signed by Jive Records, and a year later her debut single was released. "Baby One More Time" revolutionized the teen-pop scene, and Britney became an overnight superstar. The song itself, with the unmistakable first chords, was a hit, but it was the accompanying music video, with Britney in the iconic schoolgirl uniform, that truly established her image. She was viewed as innocent yet sexual, a Lolita-like figure inappropriately fetishized by the media and ruthlessly exploited by the industry. When her debut album appeared in January of 1999, Britney was not yet eighteen years old.

A string of hits followed, and somehow Britney always knew exactly what her public wanted. There were uncanny autobiographical elements in her songs, and she often addressed her struggles, albeit covertly, in her work. In "Stronger" she explored the theme of surviving; in "Lucky" she talked about a girl who seemed happy but who cried herself to sleep; in "Overprotected" and "Piece of Me" she dealt with the price of fame and of being controlled by other forces. Through it all, her fans watched her closely and got to know her intimately, though from afar. It was that unique bond that would one day help Britney to free herself from the abuses of the legal conservatorship under which she was placed in 2008. Her LGBTQ+ fans were aware that all was not well early on. In 2007, the transgender YouTube personality Cara Cunningham posted an emotional video entitled "Leave Britney Alone!" While Britney continued to release hit albums, headline sold-out concert tours, and perform a successful show in Las Vegas, privately she was going through hell.

The parallels between Britney and Judy Garland are obvious, not least because of the adulation they have both enjoyed among their queer fans. Like Judy, Britney's personal struggles have become something of a commodity. It is impossible to separate the artist from the life, the icon from the person. Where their paths will hopefully differ is the direction in which they lead. In 1969, there was little support offered to Garland, who had struggled with addiction and had been abused for most of her life. In the same way, the queer community who embraced her had a long walk along the Yellow Brick Road before they reached a safer, more accepting time. Now the future is looking much brighter for Britney, as it is also a whole different world for her LGBTQ+ fans than it was half a century ago.

At forty-one, Britney Spears is still one of the brightest stars in the music world, but perhaps more importantly, she is finally able to live her own life, freely and with agency. Her legacy as a beloved queer icon is well secured. The future is wide open—for her and for the community that played such a big part in her liberation.

In an era of instant celebrity and manufactured glamour, Lana Del Rey's appearance on the scene signaled the arrival of a new kind of artist. Suddenly, it was once again acceptable to be vulnerable, nostalgic, and even sad. Lana's old-school aesthetics, genuinely brilliant lyrics, and mysterious persona made her instantly popular among the LGBTQ+ community, especially since there has always been something of the misunderstood outsider about her. The queer cult of Lana Del Rey is a testament to the fact that, while many aspects of our culture have been embraced by the mainstream, being a misfit is still at the very heart of our identity.

When Lana Del Rey first exploded onto the scene with her baroque pop ballad "Video Games," she was accused of being inauthentic, a manufactured product of her record label. While the criticism and the ridiculing were steeped in sexist double standard, Lana refused to let the haters deter her from pursuing her passion. A decade on, she is still one of the most misunderstood and elusive artists in the industry, but there is no more doubt about her credentials: she is inarguably one of the greatest singer-songwriters of her generation, with a sizable, devoted following to prove it. The fact that many of Lana's fans are queer is telling. In her lyrics and often melancholic melodies she explores themes that reflect the community's own struggles. In many ways, she is a link that connects us with past generations of queers, who looked to their tortured divas like Judy Garland, Billie Holiday, and Marilyn Monroe for solace. Del Rey has many of the same qualities, which she writes into her music while navigating the troubled waters of the contemporary world.

Born in New York City, Lana spent most of her youth in Lake Placid, where her mother was a teacher in a local high school. A sensitive and troubled teen, she had problems with alcohol and depression, and her parents eventually sent her to a private school to get her behavior under control. Those early experiences of being misunderstood and struggling to fit in would prove instrumental in shaping Del Rey's creative persona. For a time she worked as a waitress, learning to play the guitar and discovering her own talent for songwriting. Her early performances were edgy and dark but already steeped in the kind of poetic nostalgia that would come to characterize her later work.

While a philosophy undergraduate at Fordham University, Lana started making a name for herself on the independent music scene and began working on her first album under contract to 5 Points, a small record company. It was during that time that she adopted her stage name, inspired by the glamour of the old-time movie goddess Lana Turner. Her debut release was not a success, and Lana later withdrew it from circulation and also parted ways with her record label, later signing on with Stranger Records.

"Video Games," created as a homemade video, launched Del Rey's career. The clip, which she uploaded to YouTube, introduced themes that would thereafter be closely associated with her music and aesthetic: vintage Americana; dark, melancholic descriptions of love; and poetic, nostalgia-filled lyrics. The success of the song was followed by the release of her album *Born to Die*, now considered one of the most important albums of the past two decades. While there was no shortage of controversy and criticism surrounding all aspects of her image—from her name to her look, lyricism, and voice—none of it seemed to matter to her fandom, which quickly grew. Lana's look and sound were embraced by the young generation of queers, many of whom recognized themselves in her poetic world. She was not about going out and being fabulous, loud, and happy, which has largely been the mainstream interpretation of what LGBTQ+ identity should be. Instead, she tapped into something deeper, at once darker and more profound.

With each subsequent release, Del Rey continued to grow in her artistry and her confidence, establishing a style that is uniquely hers despite being emulated by numerous artists who followed in her footsteps. *Ultraviolence*, *Honeymoon*, and *Lust for Life* all included highly conceptual, vocally ambitious songs, which earned her the respect of critics and established her as one of the most original artists of our time. Her biggest artistic success came in 2019 with the release of *Norman Fucking Rockwell!*, a collection of soft, psychedelic rock ballads with deeply personal lyrics. The album has since been hailed as one of the all-time best, with artists like Bruce Springsteen declaring Lana the best songwriter of her generation. She followed the album with her first volume of poetry, *Violet Bent Backwards Over the Grass*, which delved further into the themes included on *Norman*.

In her poetry and music, Del Rey is unafraid to show her soft, vulnerable side. She draws inspiration from nature and from iconic cultural figures of the past, and yet there is also an immediacy and a distinctive contemporary aspect to her work. She is the antithesis of the modern reality TV–bred celebrity, and she grants her listeners permission to be confused and sometimes lost in today's reality, just as she is.

"My life is my poetry, my lovemaking is my legacy."

Her latest albums, *Chemtrails Over the Country Club* and *Blue Banisters*, were both acclaimed while also attracting controversy. By this point, it seems that Lana Del Rey is not concerned with pleasing the mainstream consensus. In true queer-icon fashion, she forges her own path, staying authentic to her own idea of artistic exploration. And that is precisely what makes her an enduring figure in an era where the term "icon" is thrown around too easily.

LIL
NAS X

Lil Nas X has broken rules from the moment he appeared on the scene. First, he brought hip-hop into country music, ruffling feathers and causing a stir throughout the industry while at the same time scoring one of the most successful singles of all time with his hit "Old Town Road." Just as he was riding the wave of success, he created more controversy by becoming the first artist to come out while having a number one on the charts. With his unapologetic, homoerotic music videos and live performances, iconic fashion moments, and outspoken activism, he has single-handedly redefined the standards of masculinity, particularly for Black men. While his career is still in its early days, there is no doubt that Lil Nas X is here to stay, already established as an LGBTQ+ icon and, at long last, one able to fully embrace his queerness in all its shades.

Growing up in a suburb of Atlanta, Lil Nas X dreamed of one day becoming a star. Conscious of his queerness early on, he also vowed never to come out. He saw too much homophobia around him to subject himself willingly to discrimination. Nothing could have prepared him for what was in store for him, however: just a few years later, he is not only one of the biggest pop stars in the world but also a leading figure in the LGBTQ+ community, a symbol of liberation and queer identity for an entire generation.

The early days of his career followed a familiar, well-trodden path for a young Black wannabe rapper. He cultivated a tough image, with lyrics boasting about his maleness and his sexual conquests—who were, of course, female. It was a safe disguise but one that wouldn't last. The world was ready for a change, and while for previous generations of queer artists coming out spelled the end of a career, Lil Nas X would prove that the time has come when being openly gay is no longer the professional kiss of death it had been for decades.

What made his case especially significant was the fact that his coming out occurred within two of the most traditional areas of the pop culture arena: country music and hip-hop. Both have historically been especially tough on queer people, with country music additionally being less than receptive to artists of color. When he first posted his track "Old Town Road" on TikTok, the song became an instant sensation, and within weeks it charted on Billboard Hot Country Songs. What followed will forever be part of pop culture history. Billboard decided to remove the song from the list, deeming it "not country enough"—a move that prompted an angry reaction from various circles and accusations of racism. But the controversy proved to be just what the song and Lil Nas X needed. It quickly became a crossover hit, and with an updated version featuring vocals from Billy Ray Cyrus, it topped the Billboard chart and stayed at number one for a record-breaking nineteen weeks. The song itself was an event, but it was Lil Nas X the artist who'd make history. While he could have easily become another one-hit-wonder, Nas quickly demonstrated that he had the star quality that would lead to a major career, way beyond his impressive debut.

From the start, his musical persona raised eyebrows. He was neither a typical rapper nor a country singer. The distinctively camp elements shining through his performances and appearance prompted people to speculate about his sexuality, but unlike his predecessors like George Michael and Freddie Mercury, Nas quickly put the rumors to rest, and he publicly came out, in a true Gen Z style, via Twitter. The fact that a young, up-and-coming artist decided to come out while his first major record was still atop the charts signaled a major cultural shift; the fact that this artist was a young Black man and a rapper made it all the more significant.

The importance of Lil Nas X as a harbinger of change and a symbol of hope for the entire LGBTQ+ community cannot be overstated. The success of his music and his music videos, which feature unapologetically queer imagery, is a vital step toward equal visibility for all queer people. We have waited a long time to have that representation, and while this book opens with Judy Garland, the ultimate pre-Stonewall icon, celebrated by LGBTQ+ people who saw absolutely no one in the public eye they could directly identify with, it is a joy to end it with someone who is a full-fledged queer icon as well as being openly queer themselves. It is time to celebrate us—to celebrate our love, our lives, our contribution to society in all its areas. Lil Nas X is a queer icon of the future.

"Live your life to its fullest potential and don't really care too much about what other people think of you."

Greta Garbo — The Swedish-born Hollywood legend has been a venerated icon of the LGBTQ+ community since the 1930s.

Cary Grant — Devilishly handsome and queer himself (though in the closet, naturally), Grant enjoyed a gay following for most of his career.

Vivien Leigh — The impossibly beautiful actress is an icon in the community, both for her dramatic roles (particularly as Blanche DuBois in *A Streetcar Named Desire*) and troubled personal life.

Gloria Swanson — Her performance as Norma Desmond in *Sunset Boulevard* will forever be a queer staple of camp perfection.

Rock Hudson — Perhaps the most famous of classic Hollywood's closeted gay men, Hudson was the first high-profile celebrity to die of AIDS.

Doris Day — The iconic singer became a major icon in the lesbian community after her role as Calamity Jane and her hit "Secret Love."

Truman Capote — He is one of the most prominent queer figures in American literature.

Maria Callas — The ultimate tragic yet fabulous diva, she has been adored by the queer community since the 1950s.

Donna Summer — Once one of the biggest gay icons, her reputation in the community suffered after she allegedly made antigay remarks at the height of the AIDS crisis.

Gloria Gaynor — The disco queen gave us the iconic "I Will Survive."

Dolly Parton — A beloved figure in the queer community, she has a drag-friendly style and an endless string of hits, including "Coat of Many Colors."

Janet Jackson — Miss Jackson has proven herself to be a major queer icon on numerous occasions and still enjoys a devoted following.

Kylie Minogue — Although she never managed to achieve the same level of success in the United States as she has in Europe and her native Australia, Kylie is still without a doubt one of the most important gay icons of her generation.

Mariah Carey — The over-the-top diva with a voice to match, Carey has been a favorite of gays for three decades.

Christina Aguilera — With her campy aesthetics and powerful vocals, Aguilera is one of the most iconic singers of the past two decades, and her hit "Beautiful" continues to resonate with the LGBTQ+ community.

ACKNOWLEDGMENTS

This book has been a work in progress for a long time. By writing it I wanted to pay tribute to the icons who have meant a lot to me, and who, I am certain, have meant a great deal to many other queer people over the decades and all over the world. This is my thank-you to all of them and to those who aren't mentioned here but who have nonetheless contributed to making our world a more open and more loving place.

I would like to extend a heartfelt thanks to Kevin Stevens and the entire team at Imagine/Charlesbridge for taking this project on and giving it a loving home. To my agent, Lee Sobel, for always pushing me and making me believe I can write anything I want to—thanks for everything, Lee.

From the moment I conceived the idea for this book I envisaged only one artist for the illustrations—and I couldn't be more thrilled and grateful that he agreed to be part of this journey. Alejandro Mogollo, thank you for your immense talent and your kindness. I feel honored to have my words appear alongside your art.

Finally, to the people who make it possible for me to do what I love, my friends and my family—be it blood or otherwise—I love you and I am grateful for your love. Special thanks to Steph Brandhuber, Abaigh Wheatley, Greg Windle, Kendra Paul, Tony Walsh, Olivia Doutney-Joel, and Jeremy Kinser. Last but certainly not least, to my partner in crime and everything else, to my Sylvain—thank you.

ABOUT THE AUTHOR

ANTHONY UZAROWSKI is the author of *Jessica Lange: An Adventurer's Heart* (2022) and coauthor of *Ava Gardner: A Life in Movies* (2017). He has written numerous articles on cinema and the arts, with his work appearing in the *Guardian*, *Film International*, *Gay Times*, *Queerty*, and many other publications. You can also see his head pop up in the occasional documentary, where he shares his love for classic movies and its stars.

ABOUT THE ILLUSTRATOR

ALEJANDRO MOGOLLO DÍEZ is a Spanish artist and illustrator from Seville. He studied art, film, and photography at Cornell University before becoming an art director and graphic designer. His unique illustrations, inspired by classic Hollywood and pop culture, have garnered the attention of many celebrities, including Madonna, who has shared his work on social media. His work has been previously featured in *Encyclopedia Madonnica* and *MLVC60*